THE COMPLETE GERMAN COOKBOOK

350+The Best Recipes from Around The World: Delicious Modern Traditional German Cooking Made Simple with Authentic German Recipes.

BY: MASON P. LEONARD

TABLE OF CONTENTS

INTRODUCTIONS

RECIPES

CHAPTER-1 10

TOP 10 TRADITIONAL GERMAN FOODS 10

BROT & BROTCHEN 10

KÄSESPÄTZLE 10

CURRYWURST 10

KARTOFFELPUFFER & BRATKARTOFFELN 11

ROULADEN 11

SCHNITZEL 11

EINTOPF 11

SAUERBRATEN 12

BREZEL 12

SCHWARZWALDER KIRSCHTORTE 12

CHAPTER-2 13

BREAKFAST AND BREAD 13

GERMAN APPLE PANCAKE 13

GERMAN POTATO PANCAKES (GLUTEN-FREE) 14

GERMAN PANCAKES WITH BACON (YORKSHIRE PUDDING) 14

FARMER'S BREAKFAST (BAUERNFRÜHSTÜCK) 15

HOPPLE POPPLE GERMAN BREAKFAST CASSEROLE 16

GERMAN WAFFLES 17

GERMAN EGGS IN MUSTARD SAUCE 18

SCHNECKEN 19

WEISSWURST – WHITE SAUSAGE 21

GERMAN APPLE CUSTARD CAKE RECIPE WITH CREME FRAICHE 22

BAUERNBROT GERMAN FARMER'S BREAD 24

CHRISTMAS STOLLEN AMISH FRIENDSHIP BREAD 25

GERMAN BREAD (AUTHENTIC VOLLKORNBROT) 26

GERMAN SOFT PRETZELS (LAUGENBREZEL) 27

GERMAN BROTHER ROLLS 29

HEFEZOPF – BRAIDED SWEET BREAD 30

GERMAN BREAD ROLLS WITH SEEDS & NUTS 31

APFELMUSHÖRNCHEN: GERMAN APPLESAUCE QUARK CROISSANTS 33

GERMAN POTATO BREAD 34

BRÖTCHEN (GERMAN BREAD ROLLS) 35

GERMAN BREAD ROLLS ('WEIZENBRÖTCHEN') 36

CHAPTER-3	**38**
APPETIZERS	**38**
OKTOBERFEST GERMAN BEER CHEESE SPREAD	38
GERMAN CHEESE PLATTER	38
LIMBURGER CHEESE SALAD	39
OKTOBERFEST RADISH	40
GERMAN RED HERRING SALAD (ROTER HERINGSSALAT)	40
SMOKED TROUT DIP	41
BAVARIAN SAUSAGE SALAD WITH CHEESE	42
GERMAN COLESLAW RECIPE	42
GERMAN FRIES (BRATKARTOFFELN)	43
POTATO PANCAKES (GERMAN KARTOFFELPUFFER)	44
GERMAN MEATBALLS	45
GERMAN ONION PIE {ZWIEBELKUCHEN}	46
BEER BRAT BITES	47
SAUERKRAUT BALLS	48
GERMAN SAUERKRAUT SOUP (SAUERKRAUTSUPPE)	49
HOMEMADE GERMAN PRETZELS	50
GERMAN FRESH CREAM OF TOMATO SOUP RECIPE	51
BROILED GRAPEFRUIT WITH HONEY YOGURT AND GRANOLA	52
GERMAN POTATO SALAD	53
GERMAN CUCUMBER SALAD	54
CHAPTER-4	**55**
POULTRY	**55**
HÄNCHEN-SCHNITZEL (CHICKEN SCHNITZEL)	55
GERMAN CHICKEN FRICASSEE RECIPE	56
HOMESTYLE AND PAN-SEARED GERMAN CHICKEN SCHNITZEL	57
HÄHNCHENKEULEN: GERMAN CRISPY BAKED CHICKEN DRUMSTICKS	58
CHICKEN SCHNITZEL	58
GERMAN CHICKEN	59
OKTOBERFEST ROAST CHICKEN	60
GERMAN-STYLE CHICKEN SCHNITZEL	60
GERMAN CHICKEN SCHNITZEL	61
CHICKEN FRICASSEE	63
CHICKEN SCHNITZEL	64
OKTOBERFEST ROAST CHICKEN 'WIESNHENDL'	66
CHICKEN SCHNITZELS & GERMAN-STYLE POTATO SALAD	67
CHAPTER-5	**69**
PORK DISHES	**69**
BEST GERMAN SCHNITZEL (SCHWEINESCHNITZEL)	69

3 | P a g e

SCHWEINEBRATEN - GERMAN PORK ROAST 70

GERMAN PORK KNUCKLE (SCHWEINSHAXE) – SLOW-ROASTED WITH CRISPY CRACKLING! 71

GERMAN KASSELER: A CURED AND SMOKED PORK LOIN 73

GERMAN WHOLE HOG (SPANFERKEL) 74

SCHAUFELE RECIPE 76

SCHWENKBRATEN (GRILLED GERMAN PORK CHOPS) 77

HOMEMADE BRATWURST 78

SAUMAGEN – STUFFED PIG'S STOMACH 79

GERMAN MEATBALLS 80

PORK SCHNITZEL RECIPE 81

GERMAN PORK ROAST 82

GERMAN PORK LOIN – SLOW COOKER 82

CHAPTER-6 84

BEEF AND LAMB 84

OMA'S ROASTED LAMB RECIPE: LAMMBRATEN 84

GERMAN MEATLOAF 85

BAUERNTOPF – GERMAN ONE-POT BEEF & PORK STEW 86

AUTHENTIC GERMAN GOULASH RECIPE 87

AUTHENTIC GERMAN SAUERBRATEN RECIPE 88

GERMAN STYLE BEEF 89

LAMB SAUERBRATEN 90

PICHELSTEINER (BAVARIAN STEW) 91

GRANDMA'S LAMB SHANKS IN A WINE SAUCE 93

CLASSIC, SAVORY SHEPHERD'S PIE (WITH BEEF AND LAMB) 94

BEST FRIKADELLEN- GERMAN MEATNALLS 96

GERMAN MEATBALLS IN WHITE SAUCE (KÖNIGSBERGER KLOPSE) 98

CHAPTER-7 100

SEAFOOD 100

GERMAN FISH BALLS WITH GREEN SAUCE 100

GERMAN BAKED COD IN MUSTARD CREAM 101

FISCHBRÖTCHEN 102

GERMAN BRAT SEAFOOD BOIL 103

BIER FISCH (GERMAN BEER FISH) 103

FISCHBRÖTCHEN: GERMAN COD SANDWICHES 104

SAILOR'S SWEETHEART 105

FISH CAKES WITH HERBED SAUCE (GERMAN) 106

BREMER- GERMAN FISH SANDWICH (FISCHBRÖTCHEN) 108

GERMAN FISH MEATBALLS WITH GREEN SAUCE 108

FISH CAKES WITH CUCUMBER YOGURT ('FISCHKÜCHLE MIT GURKENJOGHURT') 110

GERMAN PLUM DUMPLINGS (ZWETSCHGENKNOEDEL) 111

GERMAN BIENENSTICH (BEE STING CAKE) 112

BLUSHING MAID - GERMAN RASPBERRY DESSERT 114

Strawberry Rhubarb Trifle 115

Sweet Venison Cake 116

German Fruit Flan Recipe..117

KOKOSMAKRONEN (GERMAN COCONUT MACAROONS)...117

Easy German Rum Balls (Rumkugeln) 118

Authentic German Cheesecake 119

Spaghetti Ice Cream 121

PRINTABLE RECIPE BELOW 121

Linzer Cookies 123

German Rice Pudding - Milchreis 124

Pfeffernusse German Pepper Nut Cookies 124

THE END **126**

INTRODUCTIONS

What comes to mind when you consider German food? Yes, German cuisine includes sauerkraut, bratwurst, Black Forest Cherry cake, and copious amounts of beer.

However, that would be a significant oversimplification and generalization because modern cookery has moved toward lighter fare, resurrecting regional German cuisines. It is generally known that Germans value healthy cuisine that is expertly cooked and presented. German cuisine is sure to impress everyone who enjoys a delicious dinner.

While typical German fares like dumplings, Wurst, pastries, and beer may give the impression that Germany is the worst country in the world to eat healthfully, restaurants offer foreign cuisine and neue Küche (contemporary cuisine). Italians and Turks, many of whom first arrived in Germany as "guest workers," run restaurants reflecting their culinary traditions. Chefs trained in Switzerland, France, or Italy return to Germany to open Continental restaurants. With corned beef, potatoes, beets, herring, and eel soup in the north and Spargel, Braten, Spätzle, and Brotzeit, a late breakfast with those beautiful brown bread and Wurst in the south, there are many contrasts in cooking customs.

In that order of popularity, Germans choose hearty meals that include meat, such as pig, beef, and fowl. The typical German eats up to 72 pounds of beef annually. Meat is typically cooked in a saucepan and eaten as sausages. In Germany, there are more than 1500 different varieties of sausage.

Breakfast (Frühstück) is frequently made up of bread, toast, and bread rolls with jam ("Marmelade" or "Konfitüre"), marmalade, or honey, eggs, and strong coffee or tea (milk, cocoa, or juice for kids). The terminology for these items varies significantly by region. Various cheeses and deli meats like ham, salami, and salted meats are also frequently consumed on toast in the morning. Breakfast also includes a variety of meat-based spreads, including Leberwurst, which is liver sausage.

The main meal of the day has traditionally been lunch, or Mittagessen, which is had around noon. In contrast to breakfast, dinner (also known as Abendbrot or Abendessen) was always a smaller meal, frequently consisting solely of a variety of bread, meat or sausages, cheese, and some sort of vegetable. Sandwiches were also possible. However, over the past 50 years, eating patterns have evolved in Germany and other regions of Europe. Many people now simply have a modest meal at work in the middle of the day and have dinner with their families at home in the evening.

Although they can also be served as a side dish, vegetables are frequently consumed in stews or vegetable soups. Many people eat carrots, turnips, spinach, peas, beans, and cabbage. Throughout the nation, fried onions are a popular accompaniment to numerous meat meals. Despite being a significant diet component, Germans typically do not classify potatoes as vegetables. In Germany, asparagus, especially the white variety known as Spargel, is frequently eaten as a side dish or as the main course. When the time is proper (late spring), restaurants may occasionally dedicate an entire meal to Spargel.

Noodles, the alternative side dish, are often thicker than Italian pasta. Spätzle, a type of noodle with many yolks, is particularly popular in the southwestern region of the nation. In addition to noodles, particularly in the south, potatoes and dumplings (Klöße or Knödel) are widely consumed. The most typical way to serve potatoes is boiled in salt water, but they are also traditionally served mashed or fried, and french fries have recently gained popularity.

Beer and wine must be mentioned when discussing beverages. All of Germany consumes a lot of beer, which is produced by numerous small and large regional brewers. Typically, it is both reasonably priced and of high quality. German beer is unparalleled in terms of variety and quality. Germany's neighboring states have rich beer-making history, but Bavaria is home to the oldest brewery in the world. Berlin, Hamburg, the Ruhr, Hesse, and Stuttgart are also the locations for producing export beers and the somewhat more bitter Pils, the most common variety of beer. Altbier, a very old brewer's artifact, is being assembled and sold today all over Germany.

The inherent lightness and subtle harmony of sweetness and acidity that characterizes good German wine are well known. Most vineyards grow on steep hillsides that are shielded from strong winds by hills that are close by that are forested, particularly along the banks of the Rhine and Mosel rivers and their branches. The warmth reflected off the sun-lit water benefits the grapes. German wines are known for their distinctive fresh, fruity acidity, which is a result of the grapes' late maturation.

In Germany, a wide range of cakes are manufactured, with fresh fruit being the most popular ingredient. Cakes frequently contain apples, plums, strawberries, and cherries. Another well-known cake is Schwarzwälder Kirschtorte, sometimes known as Black Forest Cake. Berliner or Krapfen are regional names for German doughnuts, often balls of dough with jam or other fillings inside. German chocolate cake is a tiered chocolate cake with a coconut-pecan icing filling and topping. Despite its name, this cake is not a typical German treat. A housewife contributed the original recipe to a Texas newspaper in 1957. It used Baker's German's Sweet Chocolate, which was developed in 1852 for the Baker's chocolate brand by an Englishman by the name of Samuel German. The apostrophe was mistakenly omitted in later publications, leading to the creation of the familiar German Chocolate Cake.

The German diet includes a lot of bread, typically consumed for breakfast and as sandwiches in the evening rather than as a side dish for the main course. Words like Abendbrot (meaning Evening Bread) and Brotzeit (literally Bread Time) highlight the significance of bread (Brot) in German cuisine. The inability to locate decent local bread is one of the main complaints of German expatriates in many parts of the world. Around 6,000 different types of bread and 1,200 different types of pastries are produced by German bakeries.

Nearly every (non-main) meal includes bread. A balanced diet should consist of bread, which is not considered a side dish.

Germany's most popular breads are:

- Rye-wheat ("Roggenmischbrot")
- Toast bread ("Toastbrot")
- Whole-grain ("Vollkornbrot")
- Wheat-rye ("Weizenmischbrot")
- White bread ("Weißbrot")
- Multi-grain ("Mehrkornbrot")
- Rye ("Roggenbrot")
- Sunflower seed ("Sonnenblumenkernbrot")
- Pumpkin seed ("Kürbiskernbrot")
- Onion bread ("Zwiebelbrot")

Vollkornbrot and Schwarzbrot are darker, rye-heavy bread typical of German cooking. Steamed bread, known as pumpernickel, is famous worldwide, although it is not a specific example of German black bread.

There are countless diverse foods and drinks, many unique to specific German regions. There are numerous of these foods that are probably unique to Germany. Find many German dishes here, from well-known staples to unexpected regional favorites.

CHAPTER-1
TOP 10 TRADITIONAL GERMAN FOODS

BROT & BROTCHEN

All around the nation, people eat bread in the shape of loaves (Brot) or small, typically crusty rolls (Brötchen), which is an essential component of German cuisine. Most meals include bread, particularly breakfast, dinner, and lunch (which is frequently served with rolls on the side and is typically regarded as the main meal of the day).

Grain, Pumpernickel, rye, and white bread are among the many types of bread that Germans like to eat. Compared to bread from Italy, Spain, or France, German bread tends to be heartier and heavier.

KÄSESPÄTZLE

Käsespätzle is a southern German meal produced by piling little Spätzle noodles with grated cheese and frying onions. It frequently comes with a salad, although it can also be eaten with applesauce.

Those migrating to Germany from the US or the UK will discover that this is the closest thing to macaroni and cheese they will encounter, and they will undoubtedly find that it has more taste and depth than their meal back home.

CURRYWURST

Many towns and cities sell currywurst from street vendors and fast food restaurants, and if you want to know what dish the capital city of Berlin is known for, you will immediately learn that it is currywurst.

It is a food Germans consume "on the go," not something they prepare and enjoy at home. Even though it has little nourishment, this platter of shredded sausage, chips, and hot ketchup sauce is a favorite dish in Germany, especially after a few pilsners.

KARTOFFELPUFFER & BRATKARTOFFELN

A Kartoffelpuffer is a shallow-fried pancake made with grated potatoes, egg, and flour, similar to a Swiss 'Rosti'. It is occasionally consumed in Germany for breakfast along with eggs and bacon, as a side dish with meat at lunch or dinner, or with applesauce.

On the other hand, bratkartoffeln are more similar to sauté or hashed potatoes, where little chips or chunks of potato are parboiled and then fried with onion and occasionally bacon. Again, you can eat bratkartoffeln for breakfast, lunch, or dinner.

ROULADEN

In the traditional German roulade, small slices of beef or veal are wrapped in pickles and bacon. It is typically served with gravy, mashed potatoes, cabbage, and dumplings.

It is not regionally unique, although roulade is frequently eaten when families join together for a meal during a holiday or celebration. In actuality, the name is derived from French origins.

SCHNITZEL

Tenderized meat (such as chicken, beef, veal, or pork) is covered in egg, flour, and breadcrumbs before being fried in oil to create a schnitzel. Although the Schnitzel is sometimes compared to a French escalope, it is an Austrian dish.

This dish is an excellent illustration of typical German cuisine offered in pubs, restaurants, and fast food outlets. Fries and schnitzel are a trendy and pleasant combination.

EINTOPF

A one-pot stew known as an Eintopf can contain many ingredients. It is a complete meal that often includes broth, potatoes, vegetables, and meat. It is typically eaten with bread and occasionally contains legumes like lentils.

An Eintopf is a popular food enjoyed nationwide, but the flavors and ingredients used to make it vary significantly by area. It is one of the most straightforward

German recipes and is frequently eaten at home as a family dinner. This is arguably one of the simplest German dishes, so those just starting in the kitchen might want to start with it.

SAUERBRATEN

German pot roasts are called sauerbraten, which means "sour roast" in English. The sour component refers to the meat being pickled in a sauce similar to a sweet and sour gravy before being slowly roasted in a dish.

Meats are often made of veal, beef, or pork and are first marinated for several days or even weeks. It can be found all over Germany and other German-speaking nations.

BREZEL

Pretzels are known as "bezel" in German, though you may see them marketed under either name. A Brezel is prepared by folding a long strip of dough into a knot, boiling it, and baking it. It is sold at bakeries and on street vendors. The outcome is a soft fluffy interior with a chewy brown outside.

It is then frequently seasoned with cheese, nuts, or salt before being served with a mustard dip. Brezels have a long history of being used in Christian ceremonies, and many people see the knot shape as a representation of the holy trinity, even though their origins are hotly debated.

SCHWARZWALDER KIRSCHTORTE

A mouthwatering cake is known as a Black Forest Gateau. Cherries, jam filling, and cream are all part of this chocolate sponge cake. The Black Forest, where it is from, is in southwest Germany, as suggested by the name.

In Germany, drinking coffee and eating cake in the afternoon, or "Kaffee und Kuchen," is a popular custom, particularly on the weekends when families are present. This is the season when Schwarzwälder Kirschtorte is frequently consumed.

CHAPTER-2
BREAKFAST AND BREAD

GERMAN APPLE PANCAKE

Ingredients

- ½ cup of unbleached all-purpose flour
- 1 tbsp granulated sugar
- ½ tsp table salt
- Two large eggs
- ⅔ cup of half-and-half
- 1 tsp vanilla extract
- 2 tbsp unsalted butter
- 1¼ pounds Granny Smith (3-4 large apples), peeled, quartered, cored, and cut into ½-inch-thick slices
- ¼ cup of light
- ¼ tsp ground cinnamon
- 1 tsp lemon juice
- Confectioner's sugar for dusting

INSTRUCTIONS

1. Set the upper-middle oven rack and heat the oven to 500° (425° if using cast iron).
2. Mix the flour, salt, and granulated sugar in a medium bowl. Mix the eggs, half-and-half, and vanilla in a small bowl. Mix the dry components with the liquid ones for around 20 seconds to ensure no lumps. Place aside.
3. In a 10-inch ovenproof skillet set over medium-high heat, melt butter until it sizzles. Add cinnamon, brown sugar, and apples. Cook the apples, continuously stirring, for about 10 minutes (or for about 6 minutes if using cast iron). Lemon juice is added after the heat is turned off.
4. Swiftly and carefully pour batter over the center of the pan before carefully pouring it around the perimeter. Put the skillet in the oven and immediately lower the heat to 425 degrees. About 18 minutes should be needed to bake the pancake until the edges are golden brown, fluffy, and higher than the edge of the skillet.

5. With a rubber spatula, remove from the oven and loosen the edges. Confectioners sugar should be sprinkled before flipping onto a big plate or serving dish. Slice into four wedges, then do it right away.

GERMAN POTATO PANCAKES (GLUTEN-FREE)

INGREDIENTS

- 500g Parboiled Potatoes
- 1/4 cup of White Onion – finely chopped
- 1/4 tsp Salt
- 1 tbsp Potato Starch
- 1 Egg
- 1 tbsp Ghee
- 1 tsp Olive oil

INSTRUCTIONS

1. Cooking times for parboiled potatoes vary depending on their size. The potatoes must be tender enough to penetrate with a fork easily but not too soft to be mashed.
2. Peel the potatoes if they were boiled in their skins.
3. Use the more significant grating setting to grate the parboiled potatoes.
4. Add the egg, potato starch, salt, and onion mixture. Mix thoroughly.
5. Ghee and olive oil are heated in a pan.
6. Divide the potato mixture into 6 pieces while the pan is cooking. Create pancake-like forms.
7. On medium-high heat, make the pancakes. When the first side is golden brown, flip it over and continue cooking until both sides are golden brown. Avoid packing the pan.

GERMAN PANCAKES WITH BACON (YORKSHIRE PUDDING)

INGREDIENTS

- 1 pound bacon
- 1 cup of flour
- 1 cup of milk
- Six eggs

- ¼ stick butter
- ½ tsp. salt

INSTRUCTIONS

1. After cooking the bacon, transfer the drippings to a little pitcher.
2. Set the oven's temperature to 425.
3. Mix the milk and flour in a medium pitcher. One egg at a time, whisk in. As you prepare the fat, let the meat rest at room temperature.
4. Place a sizable cookie sheet on top of nine ceramic bowls. 12 pat of butter should be added to every bowl. Pour bacon grease over the top, dividing it among the bowls in an even layer. Once the fat has melted, place the pan in the oven.
5. After taking the pan out of the oven, evenly distribute the batter among the bowls. Put the pan back in the range. 15 to 17 minutes of baking.
6. Serve with a dash of salt or, if necessary, syrup.

FARMER'S BREAKFAST (BAUERNFRÜHSTÜCK)

Ingredients

- 600 Desiree potatoes, peeled, sliced
- 120 bacon, diced
- One tbsp olive oil
- 3eggs
- ¼ cup of (60 ml) milk
- One tsp fresh chopped oregano
- salt and pepper
- 1 tbsp finely sliced chives

Instructions

1. The following recipe has undergone testing and editing by SBS Food and may not match the podcast exactly.
2. Bring salted water to a boil in a saucepan. Add the potato slices, reduce the heat to a simmer, and cook for 13 to 15 minutes or until the potato is cooked.
3. Sauté the bacon for 2 minutes over medium-high heat in a sizable frying pan. Slices of cooked potato are added, and they are simmered for 10 minutes while being frequently stirred.

4. In the meantime, stir the milk, oregano, salt, and pepper into the eggs. Together nicely.
5. Pour the mixture over the potato after lowering the heat to medium-low. Use a wooden spoon to gently stir the potato and egg mixture for 2 to 3 minutes or until the egg is cooked.
6. Serve right away after adding chives.

HOPPLE POPPLE GERMAN BREAKFAST CASSEROLE

INGREDIENTS

- 2-1/2 - 4cup of frozen hash brown potatoes
- 1/3cup of chopped onion
- 3 -4tbsp butter
- 5 -6 eggs
- 1/2 cup of milk
- mixed Italian herbs (basil, oregano, parsley, garlic powder)
- 1/2 tsp salt
- 1/2 tsp pepper
- 25 slices pepperoni
- 1 cup of shredded sharp cheddar cheese
- 1 cup of shredded mozzarella cheese

Instructions

1. Mix potatoes, onion, and butter in a sizable electric skillet over medium-high heat. Sauté until potatoes are just beginning to brown. In a pan, spread evenly.
2. Mix the eggs, milk, and seasonings in a mixing bowl. Pour over the pan of potato mixture.
3. Pepperoni should be placed on top. The eggs will be "set" after 10-15 minutes of cooking over medium-low heat with the lid on. While that's cooking, put together a straightforward fruit tray or salad.
4. Remove the cover, add the cheeses, and replace it. However, turn off the heat. Allow to stand for two to three minutes. Make toast now if you have it with this.
5. Serve right away after cutting into wedges or squares.

6. Alternative: Fry Italian bulk sausage made of pig (or turkey), drain grease, and mix with potatoes. Add some Ro-Tel tomatoes from a can. Alternatively, experiment with different cheeses!

GERMAN WAFFLES

INGREDIENTS

- 2-3/4 cup of (350 g) unbleached all-purpose flour
- 4 tsp baking powder
- 3/4 cup of (170 g) butter, softened (1-1/2 sticks)
- 3/4 cup of (150 g) organic cane sugar
- Three eggs at room temperature
- 1 tsp vanilla extract
- 2 cups of water at room temperature

INSTRUCTIONS

1. Mix the dry ingredients: Using a whisk, mix the flour and baking powder in a medium bowl. Place aside.
2. Put the butter and sugar in the bowl of a stand mixer or a hand mixer with a big mixing basin to cream the two together. For several minutes, whip the mixture at medium-high speed until it is light and fluffy.
3. Add the vanilla and eggs afterward: One at a time, add the eggs, beating well after every addition (stopping occasionally to scrape down the sides). Mix in the vanilla extract after adding it.
4. Mix the batter: Add water and the flour mixture. Until smooth and mixed beat at a low pace.
5. Making waffles: The waffle maker should be heated. As directed by the manufacturer, pour batter into the preheated waffle machine and cook until golden.
6. If you want to keep the waffles warm while you finish cooking, place them in an oven set to 200 degrees Fahrenheit (90 degrees Celsius). Directly on the oven rack or a baking sheet with a wire baking rack inside will keep the waffles crispy. Don't pile! Place on the shelf in a single layer to allow for air circulation to maintain the crispy exterior.

GERMAN EGGS IN MUSTARD SAUCE

Ingredients

- Eight large eggs
- 2 tbsp butter
- 30 g/ 1 oz/ ¼ cup of all-purpose flour
- 250 ml/ 8.5 fl. oz/ 1 cup of vegetable broth
- 100 ml/ 3.4 fl. oz/ ⅓ cup of heavy/double cream
- 2 tbsp Dijon mustard
- 1 tbsp fresh lemon juice
- Two pinches sugar
- 4 tbsp chopped dill, fresh or frozen (not dried)

Instructions

Hard-boiled eggs:

1. Put the eggs in a big pot and pour water over them. After bringing the water to a boil, turn off the stovetop. Allow standing for 12 minutes covered.
2. To halt the frying of the eggs, place them in a colander and rinse them under cold water. Peel and cut the eggs in half after cooling them for a few minutes.

Mustard sauce:

1. In a pot big enough to hold all the eggs at once, start melting the butter.
2. The flour should be added to the pan and thoroughly mixed for 1 to 2 minutes or until it turns a light yellow but not too dark.
3. Begin gradually incorporating the veggie broth while constantly whisking the sauce to prevent clumping. The final mixture ought to be very smooth.
4. Heavy cream should be added; then the sauce should be cooked, stirring often, until it thickens and coats the back of a wooden spoon. It should take 5 to 8 minutes to complete that.
5. Stir thoroughly after adding the dill, sugar, lemon juice, and mustard. If required, season the food with salt, white pepper, more sugar, or lemon juice.
6. In the saucepan, add the egg halves, gently mix to coat with sauce, and then cook through for a few minutes.
7. Serve right away with a green salad and cooked potatoes.

SCHNECKEN

Ingredients
DOUGH

- One medium russet potato (about 8 ounces), peeled, cut into 1-inch pieces
- 1¼-ounce envelope of active dry yeast (2¼ tsps)
- ½ cup of (1 stick) unsalted butter, room temperature
- ½ cup of granulated sugar
- 1 tsp finely grated lemon zest
- Two large eggs, room temperature
- 3⅔ (or more) cup of s all-purpose flour
- 1 tsp kosher salt

ASSEMBLY

- Nonstick vegetable oil spray
- 2 cups of pecan halves divided
- 1½ cups of granulated sugar, divided
- 2 tbsp ground cinnamon
- ½ cup of (packed) light brown sugar
- ½ cup of light corn syrup
- ½ tsp kosher salt
- 1½ cups of (3 sticks) unsalted butter, divided
- All-purpose flour
- 1 cup of golden raisins

Instructions
DOUGH

1. In a small saucepan, bring the potato and two cups of cold water to a boil. Reduce heat, cover, and simmer for 15-20 minutes or until the potato is cooked. You should have around 1 cup of cooking liquid left over after draining the potato. With a fork, transfer the potato to a small bowl (you should have about 1 cup of it).
2. Allow the cooking liquid for potatoes to cool until it is warm but not hot (105–110°). In a small bowl, stir the yeast and 1/4 cup of the potato cooking liquid. Let stand until bubbly, about 5 minutes.

3. In the meantime, use the paddle attachment on a stand mixer to beat the butter, sugar, and lemon zest until light and fluffy, about 4 minutes. One at a time, while the motor is running, include the eggs ultimately. Switch to the dough hook and stop the mixer. Mix ingredients on low speed until mixed, then add mashed potatoes, flour, salt, and 1/4 cup of the cooking liquid for the potatoes. Increase the speed to medium and continue mixing for 8 to 10 minutes, or until the dough is incredibly soft, elastic, barely sticky, and climbing up the hook while sticking to the bottom of the bowl (if the dough is excessively humid, add 1-3 Tbsp. flour). For 60 to 70 minutes in a warm place, cover the bowl with plastic wrap and allow the volume to double.
4. Making the dough the day before allows it to rise. Cover and let stand.

ASSEMBLY

1. Spray three 12-cup of muffin tins with nonstick spray sparingly. Chop 1 cup of pecans and reserve. In a separate bowl, stir 1 cup of granulated sugar and cinnamon; leave aside.
2. In a medium saucepan over medium-low heat, mix brown sugar, corn syrup, salt, 1 cup of butter, and the remaining 1/2 cup of granulated sugar. Stir often until the butter is melted and the mixture is smooth. Every muffin cup should contain about 1 Tbsp of the caramel mixture. Distribute the remaining 1 cup of pecan halves on top. Set muffin tins aside.
3. In a small saucepan, melt the remaining 1/2 cup of butter. On a lightly dusted surface, roll out the dough and divide it into three equal pieces. One piece of dough is rolled out into a roughly 13x8-inch, 1/2-inch-thick rectangle. Brush with melted butter, sprinkle with one-third of the saved chopped pecans and one-third of the cinnamon sugar, then scatter with one-third of the raisins. It will appear a little sparse, but that's good. When rolling, pinch the seams together to seal them. Remove about a half inch of dough from every end, then cut into 12 pieces crosswise. Place the schnecken spiral-side up in the muffin tins that have been prepared. Repeat with the remaining dough, melted butter, cinnamon sugar, raisins, and chopped pecans, dividing evenly as you go, working with one piece of dough at a time.
4. In a warm location, cover muffin pans loosely with plastic wrap and set for 40 to 50 minutes or until nearly doubled in size.

5. The oven to 325 degrees. Remove the plastic wrap, then bake the schnecken for 20 to 30 minutes, turning the pans from front to back and top to bottom. Turn out onto a baking sheet lined with parchment paper right away, let cool, and then replace any pecans that may have been stuck to the pan on the schnecken.
6. Schnecken can be prepared and put in pans (don't let rise) a day in advance. Cover and let stand.

WEISSWURST – WHITE SAUSAGE

INGREDIENTS

- Two pig casings
- 250 g Veal
- 220 g Pork (i.e., from the neck)
- 250 g Bacon, no additives
- 30 g Pork Rind
- 1 Lemon, zest from it
- 20 g Salt
- 2 g Phosphate
- 20 g onion, finely chopped
- 2 g White Pepper, ground
- 1 g Ginger, ground
- 1 g Macis, ground
- 250 g crushed ice
- 30 g Parsley

INSTRUCTIONS

1. Rinse the casing to remove the salt, then place it in a dish of warm water to soak.
2. The meat should be highly chilled before being ground in a meat grinder on a medium and then in a tiny setting.
3. While you prepare the remaining ingredients, place the ground meat in the freezer for a few minutes.
4. With tap water, thoroughly clean the case inside and out. Set it aside and cover it with a lid.
5. If you don't have crushed ice, crush ice cubes in your food processor.

6. Add the parsley to the food processor and pulse it to a fine chop after removing the ice.
7. The food processor will now be filled with the meat and all other ingredients. Let it run for a minute.
8. Crushed ice should be added; then, the food processor should run a bit. In between, make sure the temperature is under 12°C/53°F.
9. Make the sausage stuffing: To make it simpler to attach the casing to the pipe, apply some oil.
10. When the casing is on the pipe, turn the hand crank until all the air is gone and some sausage emerges.
11. Into the casing, tie a knot.
12. Fill the casing by gradually turning the sausage maker's hand crank. Though you must separate the sausages later, don't pack them too tightly.
13. Make a knot at the opposite end of the sausage once it is completely packed.
14. Now cut the sausages into the desired size: 8 cm for tiny links and 10–12 cm for larger ones.
15. Don't cut the sausages apart just yet; instead, turn them to separate them or use some kitchen twine.
16. Water should be heated in a big saucepan to 75 °C (167 °F) or almost boiling.
17. Put the sausages in the water and submerge them entirely using a plate or smaller lid.
18. The sausages are ready to be removed after 30 minutes. You can now divide them up and consume them or freeze them for later.

GERMAN APPLE CUSTARD CAKE RECIPE WITH CREME FRAICHE

Ingredients

- 175 grams flour 1 cup of + 3 tbsp
- 100 grams of butter, one stick
- One egg
- 1 pinch salt
- 60 grams sugar 1/4 cup of
- butter for greasing

FOR COVERING

- Five apples, small to medium-sized
- 2 tbsp lemon juice
- 300 g sour cream 1- 1/3 cup of
- Three eggs
- 100 ml cream 1/3 cup of + 2 tbsps
- 1 tbsp cornstarch
- 75 grams of sugar and 1/4 cup of
- 1 tbsp vanilla essence

Instructions

1. Flour should be piled up on the work surface. Create a well in the center with your hand, add the broken-up softened butter, egg, salt, and sugar, and quickly mix everything to create a smooth dough. Depending on the pastry texture, you may need to add cold water, vodka, or flour. Wrap the mixture in cling film, form a ball, and chill for about 30 minutes.
2. Apples should be peeled, split in half, and the core removed. Score multiple times on the curved side of every half. Apply a lemon juice glaze. Creme fraiche, eggs, cream, cornstarch, vanilla, and sugar should all be thoroughly combined.
3. Set the oven's top and bottom heat to 170°C/340°F. Springform pan with butter. Use the dough to line the tin by rolling it out on a floured surface, forming an edge, and then pushing down firmly to seal the border. After placing the apples in the form, top them with icing. Bake for 60 to 70 minutes in the oven. Cover the cake as soon as possible with aluminum foil if it becomes too black. Remove from the oven, then allow to cool. I returned it to the refrigerator after letting it cool thoroughly.
4. Sprinkle with icing sugar.

BAUERNBROT GERMAN FARMER'S BREAD

Ingredients

For the Dough Starter

- ¾ cup of Bread flour
- ¾ cup of Rye flour
- 3 tbsp honey
- 1 ½ cup of lukewarm water
- ½ tsp instant yeast

For the Flour Mixture

- 2 ½ cups of Bread flour
- 2 tbsp caraway seeds
- 2 tsp salt
- ½ tsp instant yeast
- 1 tbsp vegetable oil plus more to grease the bowl
- Cornmeal – for the baking tray

Instructions

1. The initial ingredients should be combined in a big bowl and blended thoroughly. Allow the yeast to activate for ten minutes.
2. Mix the flour mixture of bread flour, caraway seed, salt, and instant yeast while the starter is resting.
3. Without stirring, pour the flour mixture over the starting. For at least two hours and up to five hours, cover the bowl with plastic wrap or a fresh towel.
4. Through the flour mixture, the starter will begin to bubble a little. Your loaf's flavor will be enhanced by this prolonged rest.
5. With a wooden spoon, whisk the flour mixture into the starter after adding the oil. As the ingredients come together, remove the dough to a work surface lightly dusted with flour and knead it for 10 minutes or until it is smooth and elastic. Perhaps the dough is a little sticky. Knead the dough with enough flour to prevent your hands from becoming sticky.
6. After giving the dough about 10 minutes to rest, continue to knead it for another 5 to 10 minutes.

7. Place the dough in a sizable bowl that has been lightly greased, and lightly oil the dough's surface. For around 1 1/2 to 2 hours, or when it has doubled in size, cover it with plastic wrap or a clean cloth and place it in a kitchen without any drafts. Removing the dough, sprinkle a work surface with some flour. The dough is beaten down and lightly kneaded three or four times. Form it into a ball, put it back in the bowl, cover it, and let it rise for another hour or so.

8. Set the shelf to the lowest position and preheat the oven to 425°F. In the oven, place a small metal pan that will later be used. Create a ball out of the dough by giving it a light squeeze. A baking sheet should be covered with cornmeal before the dough is placed, with seams facing down. The dough's top should be lightly oiled before being wrapped in plastic. Put off getting up for an additional hour.

9. The top of the dough should be slashed in three parallel lines, every about 1/4-inch deep, using a sharp knife or razor blade. After that, cut a second set of three lines similar to the first set. Spray some water on the dough using a spray bottle.

10.   About 1 cup of water should be added to the small pan to create steam before placing the baking sheet in the oven. Close the door right away, then bake for 15 minutes. Bake for a further 35 to 45 minutes after lowering the heat to 400°F. It should read 190°F on an instant-read thermometer placed into the center of the bread.

11.   The loaf should be placed on a cooling rack to cool.

CHRISTMAS STOLLEN AMISH FRIENDSHIP BREAD

INGREDIENTS

- 1 cup of Amish Friendship Bread Starter
- Three eggs
- 1 cup of oil
- ½ cup of milk
- 1 cup of sugar
- ½ tsp vanilla
- 2 tsp almond extract
- 1½ tsp baking powder
- ½ tsp salt

- ½ tsp baking soda
- 2 cups of flour
- 1-2 small boxes of instant vanilla pudding
- ½ cup of chopped red cherries
- ½ cup of chopped green cherries
- ½ cup of diced dried mango
- ½ cup of chopped walnuts
- 3 ounces marzipan

INSTRUCTIONS

1. The oven should be heated to 325°F (165°C).
2. Add the items to a sizable mixing basin as directed.
3. Butter two substantial loaf pans.
4. Pour half of the batter into a sugar-lined, oiled pan. Along the length of the bread, spread a strip of marzipan or almond paste. Add the remaining batter on top.
5. Bake the bread for an hour or until it comes cleanly off the sides when a toothpick is inserted in the center.
6. Sprinkle with powdered sugar after it has cooled.
7. ENJOY!

GERMAN BREAD (AUTHENTIC VOLLKORNBROT)

INGREDIENTS

- 4 -1/2 cup of einkorn flour (you can also use whole wheat, spelled rye)
- 1/2 cup of entire einkorn berries, spelled
- 1-3/4 cup of cracked einkorn berries, spelled rye
- 1 cup of whole flax seeds
- 1-1/2 cup of sunflower seeds
- 1/4 cup of sesame seeds
- 3 tsp salt
- 2 tsp active dry yeast
- 2 tbsp sugar
- 2 cups of lukewarm water
- 2 cups of buttermilk at room temperature

- 1 cup of mild beer
- Rolled oats for sprinkling

INSTRUCTIONS

1. The yeast and sugar should be dissolved in the warm water and stand for 5 to 10 minutes until foamy.
2. In the bowl of a stand mixer, mash together all the dry ingredients. (If you'd like, you can accomplish this by hand.) Add the buttermilk, beer, and yeast mixture after that. When using the bread setting , attach the dough hook and knead for 10 minutes. Scoop the batter into a sizable, non-reactive basin, lightly cover it with plastic wrap, and allow it to remain there for at least 8 hours and ideally up to 24 hours. The longer it sits, the more the whole-grain berries will soften, and the sourdough qualities will develop. Additionally, the more time it ferments, the more liquid is absorbed, decreasing the likelihood of a moist core after baking.)
3. Set the oven to 350 degrees Fahrenheit.
4. Pour the batter into a 13x4x4 Pullman loaf pan that has been well-buttered. It will be thick and sticky but not like typical bread dough. Add some oatmeal. (Note: The bread produces those lovely little square slices when baked in a Pullman loaf pan. But it also ensures that the bread's middle is thoroughly baked.) This is something I always bake without a lid.
5. For 100–120 minutes, or until the center is set, bake on the middle rack. Use an instant-read thermometer and aim for about 205 degrees F for the best and most accurate results. Before slicing the bread, allow it to cool completely on a wire rack after 5 minutes of sitting in the pan. I strongly advise using a bread slicer to produce neat, professional slices.

GERMAN SOFT PRETZELS (LAUGENBREZEL)

Ingredients

- 2 cups of warm water
- 2 (1/4 ounce) packages of rapid-rise yeast
- 2 tbsp Barley Malt Syrup
- 6-1/2 cup of bread flour
- 2 tbsp coarse salt
- 1/2 cup of (1 stick) cold butter, cut into small pieces

- 8 cups of water
- 1/2 cup of baking soda
- 1/4 cup of dark brown sugar
- 1/2 cup of pale ale beer
- Pretzel salt for sprinkling

Instructions

1. Mix the yeast, warm water, and barley malt syrup in a mixing basin. Give it 10 minutes to proof or until frothy.
2. Salt and flour should be combined in the stand mixer's bowl. When adding the butter, mix it into the flour with your fingers until it resembles coarse sand.
3. When a shaggy dough has formed, and the water has been absorbed, pour the yeast mixture into the flour/butter mixture and stir everything together.
4. Bring the bowl to the stand mixer and attach the dough hook. Mix the dough on medium speed for about 6 minutes or until it is smooth and elastic.
5. The dough should rest and rise warmly for two hours or until it has doubled. Cover the bowl with a wet towel. (Alternatively, place the dough in the refrigerator for the night. Although the dough won't be as simple, the lengthy, steady rise will let the taste develop.
6. The oven is preheated at 450 degrees.
7. The dough should be stretched into a giant (14 by 12 inch) rectangle before being sliced into twelve strips every 12 inches long and roughly 1 inch wide.
8. Starting in the middle and working your way out to the ends, roll out every piece into a rope that is 30 to 33 inches long and about 3/4 inch thick. Create a "U" shape with the string and cross the ends, pinching at the bottom of the "U" to create the pretzels.
9. Spray 2 (or 3) big baking sheets with nonstick cooking spray to prepare them.
10. Eight cups of water, baking soda, beer, and brown sugar should all be combined in a big pot set over medium-high heat. Bring to a boil, then lower the heat so it simmers.
11. One at a time, boil the pretzels for about 30 seconds or until they float. Using a perforated spatula, transfer the cooked pretzels to the prepared baking sheet. Repeat with the rest of the pretzels.

12.   Pretzel salt should be sprinkled over the pretzels before baking. • Bake the pretzels for 5 minutes, then rotate the baking sheet and bake for 5-8 minutes, or until they reveal a deep, dark brown color.
13.   Before serving, remove them from the oven and let them cool slightly on a wire rack.
14.   Serve warm with butter, honey mustard, or plain mustard! Never forget to drink an excellent beer!

GERMAN BROTHER ROLLS

Ingredients

- 2 tbsp active dry yeast
- 1 tbsp white sugar
- 2 ½ cups of warm water (110 degrees F)
- 2 tbsp shortening
- 2 tsp salt
- 7 cups of all-purpose flour
- Three egg whites, stiffly beaten
- One egg white (for egg wash)
- 2 tbsp cold milk

Instructions

1. Warm water with yeast and sugar dissolved in it should be used for mixing. Let stand for 10 minutes or until creamy.
2. Add 3 cups of flour, salt, and shortening together. For two minutes, beat with a heavy spoon or dough whisk. Egg whites are folded in. Add flour 1/4 cup at a time, working your way up to a mass of dough that starts to pull away from the basin. Onto a floured surface, turn. For 8 to 10 minutes, knead the dough, adding more flour as needed, until it is elastic and smooth with bubbles.
3. Place the dough in a sizable mixing bowl, coat it with oil, and turn the bowl to distribute the oil. Cover with a moist towel and let rise in a warm location for about an hour or until it has doubled in volume. The dough should be deflated, formed into a circle, and given 45 minutes to rise again.
4. The oven should be heated to 425°F (220°C). The dough should be deflated before being spread on a lightly dusted surface. Form the dough into 24

equal oval rolls about 3- 1/2 inches long. Place on lightly greased baking sheets, cover, and let rise for about 40 minutes or until it has doubled.

5. On the oven's bottom rack, set an empty baking sheet. To make the egg wash, whisk together the egg white and 2 tbsp of milk in a small bowl. Apply egg wash sparingly to the rising buns. The rolls should be placed in the oven right away after 1 cup of ice cubes have been placed on the hot baking sheet.

6. Remove to a wire rack, calm, and bake at 425 degrees F (220 degrees C) for about 20 minutes or until the tops are golden brown.

HEFEZOPF – BRAIDED SWEET BREAD

INGREDIENTS

- One egg medium, at room temperature
- 7 g instant yeast one sachet
- 250 ml milk 8.5 fl oz, lukewarm
- 500 g flour 17.6 oz (Germany type 550, UK bread flour, US all-purpose flour)
- 60 g sugar 2.1 oz
- 1 tsp salt
- 80 g butter 2.8 oz
- 3 tbsp almond slices optional

INSTRUCTIONS

1. The egg should be whisked in a small bowl. One tbsp of the egg mixture is removed and placed in another bowl.

2. To the warm milk, add the yeast. Allow the yeast to activate for about 10 minutes. On the surface, there ought to be a few little bubbles forming.

3. The remaining egg, yeast-milk combination, flour, butter, sugar, and salt are now combined. Use a hand or stand mixer with a dough hook and knead for five minutes. Give the dough another five minutes to rest. After that, knead the dough once more for 5 minutes. (10 minutes should be spent kneading the dough in total).

4. For at least an hour, cover the bowl with a dish towel and set aside.

5. The dough should have about quadrupled in size by then. Remove from the bowl and manually knead for about 5 minutes on a floured surface (or a non-stick baking mat).

6. Make three balls out of the dough. Please make sure the balls are the same size by weighing them. (Mine weighed roughly 260 g/9 Ounces each).
7. Create three equal-length rolls out of them now. They ought to be roughly 40 cm (16 inches) in length.
8. Place the bread on a baking sheet covered with parchment paper after braiding the rolls (see post for an example).
9. Tea towel the braid and let it rise for an additional 45 minutes.
10. Set the oven's temperature to 180 C/ 356 F.
11. Apply the remaining whisked egg to the Hefezopf using a pastry brush. On top, scatter the almonds. Thirty minutes of baking will take place in the oven.
12. Before serving, allow cooling.

GERMAN BREAD ROLLS WITH SEEDS & NUTS

INGREDIENTS

- Prepare: (auch andere Körner möglich)
- 1 ½ tbsp. sesame seeds
- 1 ½ tbsp. flax seeds
- 2 tbsp. sunflower seeds
- 2 ½ tsp. poppy seeds
- ⅓ cup of water hot

Dough

- 2 ½ cup of all-purpose flour
- ¾ cup of rye flour
- 1 tsp. salt
- 1 tsp. barley malt
- 1 tsp. Apple cider vinegar
- ¼ tsp. Caraway seeds crushed
- ¼ tsp. fennel seeds crushed
- 3 tbsp. walnuts
- ⅓ cup of quark
- 3 tsp. yeast
- 1 cup of lukewarm water

Garnish

- 2-3 tbsp. seeds of your choice

INSTRUCTIONS

1. In a stand mixer bowl, mix all the seeds with the hot water. Then, cover the bowl with a clean kitchen towel and leave it for at least three hours or overnight.
2. Then incorporate the seeds with the all-purpose flour, rye flour, barley malt, ground fennel and caraway seeds, walnuts, yeast, apple cider vinegar, and quark.
3. To blend, quickly combine. Water should be added, then kneaded for 3 minutes at low speed and 5 minutes at medium speed.
4. For around 20 to 30 minutes, cover with a clean kitchen towel and leave to rise.
5. To split the dough into eight pieces, place it on a work surface dusted with flour.
6. Every piece of dough should be formed into a ball, then lightly dusted with flour.
7. Recover the cover and give the proofing time another 10-15 minutes.
8. Roll out a flattened dough ball into a roughly 12-inch-long rectangle.
9. Place the dough, point side up, on a baking sheet covered with parchment paper after rolling it up from the small side. Repeat with all of the dough balls.
10. Choose your favorite seeds and add 2-3 tbsp to a shallow basin.
11. The bread rolls are sprayed with water, then dipped in the seeds before being placed back on the baking pan.
12. For about 30 minutes, cover and allow to rise.
13. In the interim, preheat the oven to 425°F and put a water-filled oven-safe dish inside.
14. Use a sharp knife to make three diagonal cuts into every bread roll.
15. Repeat the water spraying, then bake for about 25 minutes in the oven.
16. Allow the baking sheet to cool fully.

APFELMUSHÖRNCHEN: GERMAN APPLESAUCE QUARK CROISSANTS

INGREDIENTS

Apfelmushörnchen Dough

- 250 g all-purpose flour plus some more
- 250 g quark could also use total fat (5%) Greek yogurt if you didn't find quark
- 150 g butter at room temperature
- 100 g applesauce I love the chunky, kettle-cooked applesauce by Grandma Hoerner's
- 1 tbsp sugar

Apfelmushörnchen Filling

- 32 tbsp applesauce for the filling

Other

- One egg yolk
- powdered sugar for dusting, optional

INSTRUCTIONS

1. All the dough ingredients should be combined in a bowl. Knead the dough, either with your hands or a dough hook and electric mixer, until it is smooth and not overly sticky. It might require extra flour to stop sticking. The dough should now be tightly wrapped and placed in the refrigerator to rest for at least four hours or, better yet, overnight.
2. 350° Fahrenheit/180° Celsius (standard setting, NOT convection) is the recommended oven temperature. The dough should be divided into four equal pieces.
3. Roll out the dough into rounds that are about 12 inches (26 cm) in diameter, working with one-quarter at a time. Cut the dough into eight equal pieces like you would a pie. Add one tbsp of applesauce to the top of every slice. When utilizing Grandma Hoerner's chunky applesauce, select the bits you prefer rather than the large slices. If a little applesauce leaks out, that's acceptable. Those bits get extra caramelized, which makes them tasty.

4. Roll up every section starting at the wide end and place on parchment-lined baking pans. Two baking sheets are required because 16 can fit on a large one.
5. Brush the rolled-up croissants with egg, which has been beaten in a bowl. After moving to the oven, bake for 20 minutes at 320° Fahrenheit/ 160° Celsius before switching to convection and baking for an additional 10 minutes. Before eating, remove from the oven and let cool for a few minutes. These rolls aren't lovely, but if you like, you can sprinkle them with powdered sugar or eat them with jam.

GERMAN POTATO BREAD

INGREDIENTS

- 8 cups of bread flour plus
- 1 tbsp. instant yeast
- 2 tsp. sugar
- 2 tbsp. salt
- 3 cups of warm water
- Two eggs
- 1 pound starchy potatoes
- 1 tbsp. German bread spice optional

INSTRUCTIONS

1. German bread spice (optional) and sugar are added to a bowl along with flour.
2. Knead for about 10 minutes while adding warm water.
3. For around 20 minutes, cover with a clean kitchen towel and leave to rise.
4. Cook the potatoes in the interim.
5. Potatoes should be riced before being added to the dough, along with salt and eggs.
6. For around 10 minutes, knead the dough.
7. Add up to 4 cups of flour gradually, depending on the potatoes. The dough ought to be still soft.
8. For about an hour, cover and allow to rise.
9. In the interim, preheat the oven to 400 degrees Fahrenheit, then put a sizable heatproof basin or pan filled with water inside.

10. The dough should be added to a floured workspace.
11. It will be a sticky dough. To make the dough rounded, lightly flour it and tuck the ends under.
12. With a sharp knife, lightly sprinkle the bread.
13. For 40 to 60 minutes, bake at 400 F in a preheated oven.

BRÖTCHEN (GERMAN BREAD ROLLS)

Ingredients

- 3 cups of all-purpose flour
- 1 tsp salt
- 1/4 tsp sugar
- 2 tsp instant dry yeast
- 1-1/4 cup of water, lukewarm

Instructions

1. Salt should be added to a big mixing bowl after the flour, and everything should be well combined. Then add the instant yeast, followed by the sugar.
2. Use your hands or the spiral dough hooks on your electric mixer to knead the dough while gradually adding the water. When the dough has formed a ball and is no longer sticking to the bowl's edge, knead it. After a few minutes, add a little more water if it becomes too crumbly. Add a tiny bit more flour if it's too wet.
3. To help the dough rise, cover the bowl with a lid or dishtowel and keep it warm but out of the draft for at least an hour.
4. Sprinkle some flour on your countertop after the dough has gotten bigger. On top of that, quickly knead the dough with your hands.
5. The dough should be divided into eight pieces and shaped into bread rolls. Consistently place the "seams" near the bottom. These rolls should be put on a parchment-lined baking pan.
6. With a sharp knife, slice the bread rolls lengthwise about halfway through. Allow them to sit for an additional 15 minutes.
7. Set your oven to 420 degrees Fahrenheit in the interim. Put water in the bottom of your range in a heat-resistant basin or small pot. On the middle rack, bake the Brötchen for roughly 15 to 20 minutes or until golden brown.

8. The bread rolls should be removed from the oven and cooled. Eating them warm or cold is an option.

GERMAN BREAD ROLLS ('WEIZENBRÖTCHEN')

Ingredients

For the poolish:

- 1 gram (0.04 ounces) of fresh yeast
- 100 grams (3.5 ounces) of water at room temperature
- 100 grams (3.5 ounces) of white soft wheat flour (German Type 550)

For the final dough:

- 225 grams (8 ounces) of lukewarm water at around 35 °C (95 °F)
- 5 grams (0.18 ounces) of lard (substitute butter or shortening)
- 5 grams (0.18 ounces) of sugar
- 15 grams (0.5 ounces) bread improver for rolls ("Brotchenbackmittel," optional but highly recommended) or 5 grams (0.18 ounces) active (diastatic) or enzymatically inactive barley malt powder
- 10 grams (0.35 ounces) salt
- 15 grams (0.5 ounces) of fresh yeast
- 400 grams (14.1 ounces) of white soft wheat flour (German Type 550)

Instructions

Prepare the poolish:

1. Dissolve the yeast in the water for the poolish the night before you bake. Till there are no more dry clumps, mix with the flour. The poolish should ferment for two hours at room temperature under a plastic wrap-covered basin. Transfer the poolish to your refrigerator and keep it there for 12 to 16 hours afterward.

Assemble and knead your final dough:

1. All the components for the final dough and the poolish should be combined in a significant mixing basin, beginning with the wet ingredients. Using a machine or by hand, knead the dough. If using a device, mix the ingredients on the low setting for 2 minutes, then knead on the high for roughly 8 to 10 minutes. If using your hands, knead the dough until it is smooth and only

slightly sticky. The dough shouldn't tear even after being stretched out very thinly. If the dough splits, knead it again until it is smooth.

Rise and proof your dough:

1. After kneading, wrap your dough in plastic and let it rest in a warm place for approximately an hour or until it has doubled.
2. Set your oven to 250 °C (480 °F), ideally with a baking stone or steel inside. To create steam, place a tray of water on the oven's bottom.
3. Ten to eleven pieces of dough, every weighing around 80 grams (2.8 ounces), should be formed. Rotate the different parts beneath your palm to form balls out of them. On a baking sheet lined with parchment paper, arrange the bread rolls and cover with a wet paper towel.
4. Allow the bread rolls to rise at room temperature for 20 to 30 minutes or until well-puffed.

Score and bake the bread rolls:

1. Use a serrated bread knife to score your bread rolls just before baking. To allow for expansion, make a relatively deep diagonal incision with a straight blade. Spray some water onto your bread rolls using a spray bottle. Bake the bread rolls on a baking sheet or transfer them to a hot baking stone.
2. At 250 °C (480 °F), bake the bread rolls for 10 minutes. After 2 and 4 minutes of baking, swiftly open the oven door and softly mist the bread rolls with water to prevent their surface from setting up too quickly. Remove the water-filled baking sheet from the oven after 10 minutes, then continue baking the bread rolls for an additional 12 to 15 minutes at 210 °C (410 °F) or until they are nicely browned. When the bread rolls are still hot from the oven, spritz a little water to give them a lovely sheen. Before eating, give them at least 15 minutes to cool off.

CHAPTER-3
APPETIZERS

OKTOBERFEST GERMAN BEER CHEESE SPREAD

Ingredients

- 16 ounces (454 g) sharp cheddar cheese, cut into ½-inch cubes
- 1 tbsp Worcestershire sauce
- 1½ tsp (1.5 tsp s) yellow mustard
- One clove of garlic, minced
- ¼ tsp (0.25 tsp) salt
- ⅛ tsp (0.13 tsp) ground black pepper
- ¾ cup of (177 ml) German beer or non-alcoholic beer if you don't drink or are pregnant!

Instructions

1. In the bowl of a food processor, add the cubed cheese, and pulse ten times to chop it finely.
2. The cheese should be processed after you've added the Worcestershire sauce, mustard, garlic, salt, and pepper. Pour the beer steadily down the feed tube while processing, and process for 30 to 45 seconds or until the mixture reaches a smooth consistency.
3. Before serving, place in the fridge for at least one hour. Serve with crackers, pumpernickel bread, or pretzels. For up to five days, the spread can be stored in the refrigerator in an airtight container or covered in plastic wrap.

GERMAN CHEESE PLATTER

INGREDIENTS
Sample Assortment:

- Brie
- Obazda
- Blue cheese
- Hard cheese like Alpine Style

- Gruyere
- Radishes
- Grapes
- Butter
- Mustard
- Pretzels
- Kaiser rolls
- Farmer´s bread

INSTRUCTIONS

1. Place everything on a serving platter or a board made of wood.
2. If you're not serving it immediately, cover it with cling film and store it in the fridge.

LIMBURGER CHEESE SALAD

INGREDIENTS

- 12 Ounces of Limburger cheese
- 2 tbsp vegetable
- 2 tbsp sherry vinegar
- One small onion, thinly sliced into rings
- 2 tbsp sweet paprika (such as Hungarian)
- salt and pepper to taste
- 1 tsp caraway seeds as a finishing touch

INSTRUCTIONS

1. Place the chunks of 1/4-inch-thick Limburger cheese on a serving platter after slicing them.
2. To prepare a vinaigrette, mix the oil, salt, and pepper with the sherry vinegar. Pour it over the thinly sliced Limburger and let it marinate for about 30 minutes. (Due to the strong fragrance, you may want to chill it while marinating, perhaps even cover it with another plate or a fitting lid).
3. When ready to serve, spread some paprika on a small plate and coat the thinly sliced onion rings on one side. Then layer the paprika-coated side up onto the slices of marinated cheese.
4. Enjoy after adding a garnish of caraway seeds!

OKTOBERFEST RADISH

INGREDIENTS

- 1 Daikon radish
- 1-2 tbsp. coarse salt
- ½ tsp. coarse pepper

INSTRUCTIONS

1. The radish should be peeled.
2. Use the spiral cutter as directed by the manufacturer.
3. Put on a dish, liberally salt, and give it time to rest for about 30 minutes.
4. Remove water, then optionally season radish with freshly ground pepper.

GERMAN RED HERRING SALAD (ROTER HERINGSSALAT)

INGREDIENTS

- 1/2 pound pickled (soused) herring fillets (German Bismarck herring or matjes herring), drained and diced small
- Two medium apples, cored and diced small
- 1/3 pound cooked red beets, diced small
- One medium yellow or red onion diced small
- 4-5 German pickles, diced small (authentic German fixes are vital to the flavor, do not substitute with American holes as they have a very different taste)

For the Creamy Dressing:

- 2-3 tbsp pickle juice from the German pickles
- 1 tbsp sunflower oil
- 1 tbsp white wine vinegar
- 1 tsp sea salt
- 1 tsp sugar
- 1 tsp German yellow mustard (tastes significantly different than American yellow mustard) (optional: some also like to add a touch of horseradish)
- 1 cup of sour cream
- 1/4-1/3 cup of heavy whipping cream

- 3 tbsp German mayonnaise (tastes significantly different than American mayonnaise)
- 1-2 tbsp fresh chopped dill
- for serving: boiled potatoes, hard-boiled eggs, crusty bread

INSTRUCTIONS

1. Pickle juice, mustard, oil, vinegar, salt, and sugar should all be combined in a small bowl and whisked until emulsified, and the salt and sugar have both been dissolved. Add the mayonnaise, mustard, dill, whipping cream, sour cream, etc.
2. In a big bowl, mix the diced herring, apples, beets, onions, and pickles.
3. Once the dressing has been added to the herring mixture, carefully whisk everything together. To taste, add salt and pepper. Add a little whipping cream if the salad is too thick. You can increase the sour cream and mayonnaise in the dressing to make it more comprehensive.
4. Place some boiled egg pieces and a sprig of fresh dill on the herring salad before serving. A few rings of onion can also be added. Next to the salad, place the potatoes. Spread the herring salad on crusty bread as an alternative.

SMOKED TROUT DIP

INGREDIENTS

- 8 Ounces smoked trout fillets
- 8 Ounces of cream cheese
- 1 tbsp capers (increase by 2 tsp if you really like capers)
- 1 tsp dried dill weed
- 1 tsp paprika
- One lemon, medium-sized (for zest and juice)
- 2 tbsp fresh chives, finely chopped + 2 tsp for garnish
- salt & pepper, to taste, if needed

INSTRUCTIONS

1. Set up a food processor and let the cream cheese come to room temperature. Chop the chives finely, reserving 2 tsp for garnish.

2. Crumble the smoked trout over the top after pulsing the cream cheese to break it up. Combination procedure.
3. Pulse to blend after adding the capers, dried dill, and paprika.
4. Add the lemon's entire zest and around half of its juice. To merge, pulse one final time. Put in a mixing basin. Stir the chives in. Transfer to a serving dish, then top with the saved chives and paprika.

BAVARIAN SAUSAGE SALAD WITH CHEESE

INGREDIENTS

- 4 cups of ring bologna, finely sliced, 300g
- 2 cups of Emmental cheese, finely sliced, 200g
- 1 cup of pickles, finely sliced, 100g
- 3 tbsp vinegar
- 1-2 tbsp sunflower oil
- 3 tbsp water
- 4 tbsp brine from the pickles
- Salt, to taste
- Pepper, to taste

INSTRUCTIONS

1. Sliced ring bologna, Emmental cheese, and pickles should all be combined in a large bowl.
2. Vinegar, sunflower oil, water, and pickle brine should all be combined in a small basin. To the large bowl, add.
3. After combining everything, add salt and pepper to taste.
4. For around three hours, wrap the salad in plastic wrap and refrigerate it.
5. Serve with rustic bread and optional parsley and onion ring garnish.

GERMAN COLESLAW RECIPE

Ingredients
For the Marination

- pound Green Cabbage
- 1 Tbsp Salt. See the post for salt qualities
- ½ cup of Lukewarm Water

For the Dressing

- 2 Tbsp Apple Cider Vinegar
- ¼ cup of Oil. See the bar for a recommendation
- ½ Tsp Black Pepper Ground
- 1 Tsp Caraway Seeds Whole

To garnish

- chives fresh chopped

Instructions

1. Rinse your cabbage and throw away any tough outer layer.
2. Put the cabbage in a sizable mixing basin after shredding it.
3. The cabbage is combined with salt and warm water.
4. To remove excess water and soften the coleslaw, let it marinade for at least one hour.
5. The coleslaw should be promptly rinsed under running water, strained well, and dried with a clean kitchen towel to remove any remaining liquid.
6. In a salad bowl, mix the coleslaw with the oil, vinegar, and caraway seeds. Season to taste with black pepper.
7. As a garnish, top the slaw with some chopped chives and serve chilled.

GERMAN FRIES (BRATKARTOFFELN)

INGREDIENTS

- 2 lbs firm (waxy) potatoes such as Gold, Red Bliss, or new potatoes
- One small onion
- Six strips thick cut bacon
- 2 tbsp cooking oil
- salt and pepper to taste to season potatoes
- 1 tbsp finely chopped fresh herb (flat-leaf parsley, thyme,)

INSTRUCTIONS

1. The potatoes should be cleaned before boiling them with their skins on in salted water until they soften but still have some firmness.
2. Cut the bacon into thin strips (or dice it) and thinly slice the onions while the potatoes boil. The bacon should be cooked in a pan over medium heat until

crispy. Drain over paper towels after removing them. The onions should be cooked in the extracted fat over medium heat until they turn crispy; then, they should be taken out and set aside.

3. Check on the boiling potatoes while the bacon and onions are cooking. Pour off the hot water and run cold water over the vegetables once you can pierce them with a fork, but they are still somewhat firm.

4. The potatoes should be peeled (optional) and cut into circles, semicircles, or diced as soon as they have cooled enough to handle comfortably.

5. In the same skillet, you used to cook the bacon and onions, sauté the sliced potatoes in two batches. Per batch, add a tbsp of cooking oil. To ensure that the potatoes brown evenly, avoid packing the skillet too full. When one side is crispy, flip them over and brown the other until satisfied.

6. The crispy potatoes should be combined with the bacon, onions, and any fresh herbs of your choosing that have been coarsely chopped. Serve after seasoning with salt and pepper!

POTATO PANCAKES (GERMAN KARTOFFELPUFFER)

INGREDIENTS

- 2-1/2 pounds starchy potatoes, peeled and very finely grated (RAW, not cooked)
- One small yellow onion, very finely grated
- Two large eggs
- 1/4 cup of all-purpose flour
- 1 tsp sea salt
- neutral-tasting oil for frying

INSTRUCTIONS

1. Grated potatoes should be completely drained of liquid by being placed in a colander and squeezed with your hands or placed in a clean dish towel and drained of fluid.

2. Use your hands to incorporate the grated potatoes, onion, eggs, flour, salt, and drained potatoes into a sticky mixture. If necessary, add a little extra flour. Use the mix immediately; don't let it rest for too long.

3. A non-stick skillet should be heated over medium-high heat with a few tsp of oil. Add 1/3 to 1/2 cup of the mixture, depending on your desired size, and

flatten into pancakes with the back of a spoon. For 3 to 5 minutes, fry the Kartoffelpuffer until golden on both sides. Briefly place them on paper towels.

4. Serve hot immediately with powdered sugar, fruit compote, or applesauce. Serve the dish with meat and sauce or herbed yogurt, quark, or crème fraiche for a savory variation.

GERMAN MEATBALLS

Ingredients

For the Meatballs

- 1/4 cup of finely chopped onion
- 1 pound lean ground beef
- 1/2 pound ground pork
- 3/4 cup of plain breadcrumbs
- 1 tsp kosher salt
- 1/2 tsp ground pepper
- 2 tbsp chopped fresh parsley
- 1 tsp Worcestershire sauce
- One egg, whisked
- 1/2 cup of milk
- 2 tbsp olive oil
- 8 -ounces of bacon, chopped
- 32– ounces sauerkraut, undrained

For the Mustard Gravy

- 2 tbsp butter
- One clove of garlic, minced
- 2 tbsp flour
- 1/2 cup of milk
- 1/2 cup of chicken broth
- 2 tbsp German mustard (dijon will also work)
- Salt and pepper

Instructions

1. In a small, microwave-safe bowl, put the onion. One minute of high-power heating in the microwave. Once the onions have softened, remove, mix, and simmer for one more minute.
2. The onions, ground beef, ground pork, breadcrumbs, salt, pepper, parsley, Worcestershire sauce, egg, and milk should all be combined in a large basin. Make 2-inch meatballs out of the mixture. Place aside.
3. In a big skillet over medium heat, warm the oil. The meatballs are browned on all sides and removed from the pan. Add the bacon to the skillet after draining the oil. Drain most of the fat after cooking the bacon until it is crisp.
4. Stir in the sauerkraut after adding it to the pan with the bacon. Replacing the meatballs, cover the pan. Cook for 20 minutes, or until the meatballs are thoroughly cooked, on medium-low heat.
5. For the gravy, mix the milk and chicken broth in a small basin. Place aside.
6. Melt the butter and sauté the garlic for two minutes, or until tender, in a small saucepan over medium heat.
7. After adding the flour, simmer for two minutes. Add the milk mixture gradually while whisking until the mixture is smooth. Cook while stirring until the liquid just begins to boil and thickens.
8. Add the mustard and salt and pepper to taste.
9. Pour the mustard over the meatballs before serving.

GERMAN ONION PIE {ZWIEBELKUCHEN}

Ingredients

- One pie crust
- 2 pounds onions, sliced
- 5 ounces bacon, chopped
- 1 cup of sour cream
- Four eggs
- paprika
- salt
- caraway seeds (optional)

Instructions

1. Set the oven's temperature to 400.
2. Use pie crust to line a 9" deep dish pie plate. Place aside.
3. Cook the bacon and onions together in a skillet until the bacon is cooked through. Salt and paprika should be sprinkled on it.
4. Fill the pie crust with bacon and onion mixture.
5. Sour cream and eggs should be combined, then poured over the onion mixture. (If using, scatter some caraway seeds on top.) Forty minutes in the oven. Five minutes should pass before slicing.

BEER BRAT BITES

INGREDIENTS

- 1 package Johnsonville Bratwurst Sausages
- 1-12 ounce bottle of beer
- 1/2 cup of brown sugar
- 1 tbsp Dijon mustard
- 1 tbsp chopped parsley
- 2 tsp cornstarch

INSTRUCTIONS

1. The bratwurst sausages should be cooked to perfection in the Sizzling Sausage Grill.
2. Make the sauce while the sausages are frying. Over medium-high heat, mix the beer and brown sugar in a pot and bring to a boil. Reduce the heat, cover, and simmer the mixture for 10 to 15 minutes or until it has reduced and thickened. Add the mustard and blend well.
3. Pouring the cornstarch into the beer mixture after whisking it with 1 tbsp of cold water. Beer should be brought to a boil before cooking for one minute with constant stirring to thicken the sauce.
4. The sausages should be cut into 1-inch pieces and added to the sauce in the pot. Serve after adding parsley.

SAUERKRAUT BALLS

Ingredients

- Two bratwursts, removed from their casings, crumbled
- 4 Tbsp minced onion
- 1 (14 ounces) can think of Frank's Kraut, drained and chopped fine
- 1 cup of + 1 Tbsp seasoned breadcrumbs
- Salt & Pepper to taste
- 1/4 tsp garlic powder
- 2 tsp dried parsley
- 4-ounce cream cheese
- One heaping tsp stone ground mustard
- 1/3 cup of flour
- Two eggs
- 1/4 cup of milk
- vegetable oil for cooking

Instructions

1. In a skillet, sauté sausage and onion until the meat is fully cooked. Take out any grease. Add salt and pepper to taste.
2. Cream cheese, garlic powder, parsley, and mustard should all be combined.
3. To the sausage mixture, add 1 Tbsp of bread crumbs and sauerkraut.
4. Add the cream cheese mixture and blend with a whisk.
5. Put the food in the refrigerator to chill for a few hours.
6. Mix milk and egg in a whisk.
7. Using a cookie scoop, shape the mixture into balls. After coating in egg mixture and breadcrumbs, roll in flour.
8. Brown the balls on all sides in hot oil in a skillet.
9. Place on a piece of paper towel to absorb any extra grease.
10. Serve warm.

GERMAN SAUERKRAUT SOUP (SAUERKRAUTSUPPE)

INGREDIENTS

- 4 ounces of flavorful smoked bacon, diced
- Two medium to large yellow onions, chopped
- Two cloves garlic, minced
- 2 tbsp tomato paste
- 1 tbsp quality smoked Hungarian paprika (preferably Kalosca) (mild, not hot)
- 1/2 tsp dried marjoram (a very traditional herb in German cooking)
- 1/2 tsp caraway seeds, lightly crushed
- 1 tsp salt
- 1/4 tsp freshly ground black pepper
- 1 tsp sugar (optional)
- 4 cups of quality chicken broth (we recommend Aneto 100% All-Natural Chicken Broth)
- Eighteen ounces of German Sauerkraut drained (about 3-1/2 heaping cup). Do NOT substitute with American sauerkraut
- How to Make Sauerkraut (it's easy! Click the link for the recipe tutorial)
- 1/3 cup of crème fraîche (can substitute full-fat sour cream)

INSTRUCTIONS

1. The bacon is cooked in a soup pot until done. Add the onions and simmer for 5-7 minutes, until they are just beginning to caramelize. For one more minute, add the garlic. Cook for one more minute after adding the tomato paste and seasonings. Bring to a boil after adding the chicken broth and sauerkraut. Simmer for 20 minutes with the cover on medium heat. Creme fraîche or sour cream is then stirred and heated without boiling.
2. Serve warm with some crème fraîche or sour cream on the side. Great accompaniments include crusty bread and a salad of lush greens.

HOMEMADE GERMAN PRETZELS

Ingredients

- 4 cups of all-purpose flour
- 2 tsp salt
- 1 tsp sugar
- 1 cup of lukewarm water
- 2 pkg active dry yeast 4-1/2 tsp
- 3 tbsp butter
- Coarse salt for sprinkling
- Soda Bath
- 1/2 cup of baking soda
- 2 quarts water

Instructions

1. Activate the yeast in the warm water. Salt and flour should be combined in a sizable mixing dish. In the center of the flour mixture, create a well, and then add the sugar. Fill the well with the yeast/water combination. Before blending, let it sit for 15 minutes.
2. To make a smooth dough, mix the mixing bowl with the softened butter. To get all the dry ingredients together, I had to add tbsp of water after using the dough hook on speed 2 for around 6 minutes. After removing the dough hook, allow the dough to rest for a half-hour.
3. The dough should be divided into twelve equal pieces. Roll out every detail on a table (without using any flour because you shouldn't need it) to a length of about 20 inches, tapered at the ends. Because it's tough to get a good form with a short, thick rope of dough, please don't make it any faster than 20 inches. As you lay out the dough, it shouldn't get too warm, or it can tear.
4. Place a dough rope on a cookie sheet prepared with parchment paper and shape it into the letter "U" to form the pretzel shape. Twice cross the "U"'s" two ends over one another to create a twist. Place that twist over the bottom curve of the "U" by bringing it down.
5. Place the pretzels in the refrigerator for about an hour without covering them. This promotes the development of skin that will better absorb the dipping solution and produce a gorgeous, lustrous crust.
6. set the oven to 400 degrees.

7. Bring the water to a boil in a sizable stockpot or pasta pot by filling it 3/4 full. Add the baking soda to the hot water slowly and cautiously. When baking soda is added to the water, a reaction will occur, causing the water to bubble wildly before subsiding. Just to be cautious, take a step back. Gently place every pretzel into the bath using a slotted spoon for 10 seconds, flip them over, and continue for an additional 10. Only 10 seconds total of Astrid's call were made. Put them on a parchment paper-lined baking sheet.

8. Using a razor blade or a sharp knife, score the dough once like you would for a baguette.

9. Add some salt, coarse. Depending on how dark you like your pretzels to be, bake them for 15 to 20 minutes (my needed 20 minutes for an excellent dark crust).

GERMAN FRESH CREAM OF TOMATO SOUP RECIPE

Ingredients

- 1 tsp good-quality olive oil
- 1/2 cup of onion, chopped (1/2 medium onion)
- One clove of garlic, chopped
- 1 pound (about 8 to 10) tomatoes (preferably Roma tomatoes: quartered)
- 2 tbsp vodka
- One sprig of fresh thyme
- One sprig oregano
- 1 cup of chicken broth
- 1/2 tsp kosher salt
- Dash freshly ground pepper
- 1 tbsp fresh chopped basil for garnish
- 4 tbsp heavy whipping cream, whipped (optional)

INSTRUCTIONS

1. Half a cup of finely chopped onions should be sautéed in 1 tsp of high-quality olive oil until transparent. To avoid burning it, add one clove of chopped garlic and continue to sauté for a few minutes.

2. For 10 to 15 minutes, while stirring occasionally, add the 1 pound of quartered tomatoes, 2 tbsp of vodka or tequila, and the herbs. Cover the pan.

3. Remove from the stove after tomatoes are mushy and add ingredients to blender.
4. Place one or two hot pads on the blender's lid and hold them there while blending the hot tomatoes for about 30 seconds.
5. Then, using the back of a spoon, force all the liquids back into the pan after pouring the sauce through a sieve over the pan. Although this step is optional, the tomato soup it produces is smooth and tasty.
6. Add 1 cup of vegetable or chicken broth, as well as salt and pepper to taste. For five minutes, heat gently. Pour into bowls and top with a basil leaf garnish and a dollop of unsweetened whipped cream.

BROILED GRAPEFRUIT WITH HONEY YOGURT AND GRANOLA

INGREDIENTS

Broiled Grapefruits

- Three grapefruits (I used the sweet Texas Rio Star variety)
- 6 tbsp raw sugar or brown sugar (you'll need two tbsp of sugar per grapefruit)
- sprinkle ground ginger
- sprinkle ground cinnamon
- dash sea salt

For Serving

- Greek yogurt
- honey, for drizzling
- granola (a few handfuls)

INSTRUCTIONS

1. Heat the broiler. Slice off about 14 inches of the peel from the base end and the stem end of every grapefruit to make the bases of the halves flat so they don't move around. After that, make parallel slices through every grapefruit, cutting them in half. To remove extra moisture, lay the grapefruit halves face down on paper towels for about five minutes.
2. Mix the raw sugar, brown sugar, ginger, cinnamon, and a pinch of salt in a small bowl. I used a combination of both. The grapefruit halves should be placed face up on a rimmed baking sheet or a 139-inch glass baker. Use

roughly 1 tbsp of the sugar mixture to sprinkle every half liberally. Until the sugar is melted and turning a rich amber color, broil for 7 to 10 minutes. Serve the grapefruits warm or at room temperature with a generous dollop of yogurt (swirl in honey if you'd like) and a handful of granola after allowing them to cool for at least a few minutes.

GERMAN POTATO SALAD

INGREDIENTS

- 2 pounds waxy potatoes
- 6-8 slices bacon, finely diced
- ½ cup of finely chopped onion
- ¾ cup of beef stock
- 6 Tbsp white vinegar
- 1 tsp mustard, Dijon
- 2 Tbsp vegetable oil, sunflower
- 1 tsp sugar
- ½ tsp salt,
- ¼ tsp black pepper, freshly ground
- 2 Tbsp chopped parsley,

INSTRUCTIONS

1. Depending on the size of the potatoes, boil the potatoes for about 20 minutes over high heat in a big saucepan filled with an inch of water.
2. Make the dressing in the interim. In a pan over medium heat, cook the bacon until it is crispy. Leave the rendered fat in the pan and remove and put aside the bacon. For around 3 to 4 minutes , add the onion to the pan and sauté until transparent but not browned. Add the beef broth and boil for a while. Add the vinegar, mustard, oil, sugar, salt, and pepper after lowering the heat .
3. So that you can handle the potatoes, let them cool just a little. Potatoes must be peeled. Place the potatoes in a big basin after cutting them into 1/4-inch slices or cubes.
4. Over the potatoes, pour the heated dressing. Mix the salad, then fold the bacon pieces .To allow the potatoes to soak up the sauce's flavor, let the salad sit at room temperature for at least 20 minutes before serving.

GERMAN CUCUMBER SALAD

Ingredients

- ⅓ cup of sour cream
- ½ tsp prepared yellow mustard
- 1 tbsp white vinegar
- 1 tbsp milk
- ¼ tsp kosher salt more, to taste
- ¼ tsp black pepper more, to taste
- 2 tbsp fresh chopped dill more, to taste
- One large English cucumber washed and thinly sliced (about 2 ½ cups of sliced)
- ½ cup of thinly sliced red onion

Instructions

1. In a medium bowl, mix the sour cream (or yogurt), milk, mustard, vinegar, salt, pepper, and dill.
2. Cucumber and onion slices should be gently tossed or stirred to coat everything. 30 to 1 hour before serving, cover and chill the dish in the refrigerator.

CHAPTER-4
POULTRY

HÄNCHEN-SCHNITZEL (CHICKEN SCHNITZEL)

Ingredients

- Two large chicken breasts
- Salt and pepper
- 4 Tbsp butter, divided
- Vegetable oil
- ½ c unbleached all-purpose flour
- Two eggs, beaten lightly
- 1 ½ c plain, unseasoned breadcrumbs
- Lemon slices and fresh parsley (to serve)

Instructions

1. Cut through the side of every chicken breast as if you were butterflying it, and make two thin cutlets out of every breast. The four chicken cutlets should have pepper and salt on both sides. Please put them in between two pieces of plastic wrap and roll or mallet them thin to 1/8 inch thickness. Set aside the cutlets.
2. In a medium sauté pan, melt 2 tbsp of butter and add just enough oil to cover the bottom of the pan by 1/8 inch. Oil and butter should be heated well until they start to crackle. (Tip: To test whether the oil is ready, drop a few bread crumbs into the heated oil; if they crisp up and crackle nicely without burning, the oil is ready.)
3. Place the flour and breadcrumbs in separate shallow dishes while the oil is cooking. The beaten eggs should be put in a shallow basin.
4. Every cutlet of pounded chicken should be fully covered in flour.
5. After that, submerge the cutlet completely in the beaten eggs, letting any excess drip off.
6. Once fully covered, but without pressing the breadcrumbs into the cutlet, dip the cutlet into the breadcrumbs one last time. Allow any extra breadcrumbs to drop.

7. Transfer the breaded cutlet to the heated oil right away. Fry every side for 1-2 minutes or until golden brown. Place the cutlet on a wire rack or dish covered with paper towels.

Continue by adding more cutlets.

1. Add 2 Tbsp of butter and more oil if necessary after cooking two cutlets. Continue frying the remaining two cutlets while heating the oil/butter combination to frying temperature.
2. Slices of lemon and parsley should be added to the chicken schnitzel before serving. Serve with German potato salad, spätzle, fries, and braised cabbage.

GERMAN CHICKEN FRICASSEE RECIPE

INGREDIENTS

- 1 tbsp olive oil
- 3 tbsp butter, divided
- 8-ounce fresh white, sliced
- 1½ pounds boneless skinless chicken thighs, cubed
- 4 tbsp all-purpose flour
- 2 cups of chicken broth, hot
- 1 cup of frozen peas (optional)
- ½ cup of heavy cream,
- salt, pepper
- fresh parsley to garnish

INSTRUCTIONS

1. Oil and 1 tbsp butter should be heated over medium heat in a big pot or Dutch oven. Mushrooms should be added and sautéed for a few minutes until golden brown. With a slotted spoon, remove the mushrooms and set them aside.
2. Chicken should only be cooked briefly without browning in the remaining butter. Add flour and mix by stirring. Continue stirring while adding hot broth; turn up the heat and bring to a boil. Started the mushrooms back into the pan. For roughly 15 to 20 minutes, simmer under cover with the heat

reduced to medium-low. You can add a little more water if the sauce becomes too thick.

3. If using, add the peas and boil for 2 to 3 minutes. Put the cream in. Season. To finish, garnish with parsley.

HOMESTYLE AND PAN-SEARED GERMAN CHICKEN SCHNITZEL

INGREDIENTS

- 4 (6-ounce) skinless, boneless, thinly sliced chicken breasts
- 1/4 tsp kosher salt
- 1/2 cup of all-purpose flour
- 1/8 tsp cayenne pepper
- 1/8 tsp freshly grated nutmeg
- 1/4 cup of milk
- One large egg, lightly beaten
- 1 cup of Panko breadcrumbs
- 2 tbsp finely chopped fresh flat-leaf parsley
- 1/2 tsp garlic powder
- cooking spray
- 1 tbsp canola oil

INSTRUCTIONS

1. Set the oven to 350 degrees and cover a baking sheet with foil with a rim. Use nonstick frying spray to coat.
2. Chicken cutlets should be salted and freshly peppered.
3. Make three small dishes for dipping and dredging. 1/2 cup of flour with 1/8 tsp of cayenne and nutmeg in the first dish. Second dish: 1 softly beaten egg and 1/4 cup of milk. Panko crumbs, parsley, and garlic powder combined in the third dish.
4. Chicken cutlets should first be dredged in a flour mixture, then in a milk/egg combination, and finally in a panko mixture, shaking off any excess.
5. I heated a 12-inch cast iron skillet that was big and nonstick over medium-high heat. Swirl canola oil into the pan to coat it. 2 chicken breast halves should be added. Cook for 2-3 minutes per side until well browned. Place chicken on a baking sheet after removing it from the skillet. Continue with the remaining two chicken breast cutlets, possibly using extra oil.

6. Cook chicken in a 350°F oven for 15 minutes or until fully cooked.

HÄHNCHENKEULEN: GERMAN CRISPY BAKED CHICKEN DRUMSTICKS

INGREDIENTS

- 12 chicken drumsticks
- 4 tbsp olive oil
- 2 tbsp sweet paprika powder
- ½ tsp half-sharp paprika powder can also use chili
- 1 tbsp curry powder
- 1 tsp garlic powder
- 1 ½ tsp salt
- Three twigs of rosemary leaves were removed and finely chopped
- 1 tsp ketchup
- 1 tsp honey

INSTRUCTIONS

1. The oven should be preheated to 425 Fahrenheit (220 Celsius) on a convection setting (450 Fahrenheit or 230 Celsius on a traditional setting).
2. Rub the drumsticks with a mixture of the ingredients above.
3. 35 to 45 minutes for baking. A minimum internal temperature of 165 degrees Fahrenheit (74 degrees Celsius) is required. Good appetite!

CHICKEN SCHNITZEL

Ingredients

- 4 (6 oz) chicken breasts
- salt and black pepper
- ½ cup of all-purpose flour
- Two large eggs, beaten
- 1 cup of fresh breadcrumbs (pulse three slices of bread)
- ½ tsp garlic powder
- canola or vegetable oil for frying
- lemons and chopped parsley for serving

Instructions

1. The chicken should be pounded to a thickness of 1/4 inch when placed between two pieces of plastic wrap. Black pepper and salt should be lightly sprinkled on both sides.
2. Three pieces of bread should be pulsed in a food processor to create breadcrumbs. If you don't have fresh bread, you can also use ordinary breadcrumbs.
3. Put the breadcrumbs, egg, and flour in three separate shallow basins. Mix breadcrumbs and garlic powder.
4. Set the oven to 200 °F. Put a cooling rack for wire on a baking sheet and set it aside. In a large skillet set over medium-high heat, warm 1/4 inch of oil. Dip the chicken in the flour, the eggs, then the breadcrumbs, coating all of the chicken's surfaces and edges while the skillet heats up. Shake off any extra breadcrumbs gently.
5. Two cutlets at a time, cook for 3 minutes on every side or until golden brown. While the remaining cutlets are being cooked, transfer them to a wire rack and put them in the oven. Serve right away with freshly squeezed lemon juice and chopped parsley on top.

GERMAN CHICKEN

Ingredients

- Four skinless, boneless chicken breast halves
- 1 cup of barbecue sauce
- 22 ounces sauerkraut

Directions

1. oven to 350 degrees Fahrenheit (175 degrees Celsius).
2. Sauerkraut should be arranged in a single layer in a nine-by-13-inch baking dish. On top of the sauerkraut, place the chicken breasts. Over the chicken, drizzle the barbecue sauce. When the chicken is done and the juices run clear, bake covered in the oven for 30 minutes.

OKTOBERFEST ROAST CHICKEN

Ingredients

- One whole chicken, about 3.5 pounds
- 1 tsp salt
- 1 tsp paprika sweet
- 1/4 tsp dried thyme
- 1/4 tsp oregano
- One pinch of ground pepper
- 1/4 tsp marjoram
- One bit of ground rosemary
- 2 tbsp butter

Instructions

1. Inside and out, thoroughly wash the chicken, then pat it dry with a towel.
2. In a bowl, mix the herbs and spices. Apply the spice mixture all over the chicken.
3. In a baking dish with 1/2 inch of water, put the chicken. Place a few small pats of butter on top of the chicken. Roast until done, about one hour at 325 degrees. Every 15-20 minutes or so, while the food is roasting, baste it with the pan juices.
4. Serve with potato dumplings and red cabbage or with French fries, radish, and a German pretzel.

GERMAN-STYLE CHICKEN SCHNITZEL

Ingredients

- 4-oz. skinless, boneless chicken breasts, pounded to 1/4" thickness
- Kosher salt, freshly ground pepper
- Vegetable oil (for frying)
- 1cup of all-purpose flour
- Three large eggs, beaten to blend
- 2tbsp whole grain mustard
- 2-1/2 cup of panko (Japanese breadcrumbs)
- 1tbsp chopped fresh flat-leaf parsley
- Lemon wedges (for serving)

SPECIAL EQUIPMENT

- A deep-fry thermometer

INSTRUCTIONS

1. Chicken breasts should be salted and peppered.
2. Install a deep-fry thermometer in a big cast-iron pan or another heavy straight-sided skillet (not nonstick); add oil to a depth of 1/2"; heat over medium-high heat until the thermometer reads 315° (you want a moderate heat here because chicken breasts are so thin, they cook relatively quickly).
3. In the meantime, put the flour in a small bowl. In a different small bowl, whisk the eggs and the mustard. In a third shallow bowl, add panko. Working with one chicken breast at a time, coat in flour, shaking off excess, then gently dip into the egg mixture, rotating to coat evenly. Finally, delicately top with panko, pushing to attach firmly. Cook the chicken until golden and crisp, about 2 minutes per side, while working in 2 batches. Salt the chicken before transferring it to a wire rack inside a baking pan.
4. Serve chicken garnished with parsley and lemon wedges nearby for squeezing over. Add Lemony Mint Tabbouleh to the dish.

A SCHNITZEL ISRAELI

1. Restaurants in Israel frequently serve chicken and turkey schnitzel. Depending on the chef, the seasonings can include paprika, cumin, garlic, cumin, or cardamom, and a matzo meal can occasionally replace breadcrumbs.
2. This variation should be served with tabbouleh, lemon wedges, and tahini sauce (1/2 cup of tahini mixed with 1/4 cup of lemon juice, 1/4 cup of water, and a dash of hot sauce).

GERMAN CHICKEN SCHNITZEL

INGREDIENTS

Chicken

- 4 boneless, skinless chicken breast
- 1 tsp salt
- freshly ground pepper

Coating

- 1 cup of all-purpose flour
- 2 cups of breadcrumbs
- Three eggs beaten
- 2 TBS lemon juice freshly squeezed
- ¾ tsp Kosher salt (divided)
- freshly ground pepper

Frying

- neutral flavor oil, I prefer canola

Garnish

- 1 TBS chopped parsley flat-leaf (Italian)
- One lemon cut into rounds
- 1 TBS caper optional

INSTRUCTIONS

Chicken

1. Half every chicken breast lengthwise.
2. Cut every chicken breast in half lengthwise, making three pieces from the thicker portion of the breast.
3. Place every piece of chicken between two sheets of plastic wrap and press every detail with a mallet or other blunt object until it is approximately 1/2 inch thick and flat. - placed on a plate or cutting board
4. On both sides of the chicken, season with a bit of salt and freshly ground pepper.

Coating

1. Establish a dredging station with three distinct dishes:
2. In a bowl, whisk the three eggs. Add 1/4 tsp salt and a few grinds of pepper.
3. Flour should be added to a different bowl or pie plate along with 1/4 tsp of salt.
4. Add the bread crumbs and season with 1/4 tsp salt and a dash of pepper in a third bowl or pie plate.

5. Every chicken piece should be well coated with flour, egg wash, and bread crumbs before being placed on a dish in a single file (the chicken should not be stacked).

Frying

1. Heat 1-1/2 inches of oil on medium heat in a big frying pan.
2. Add the chicken to the hot oil in batches (do not crowd the pan) with about 2-3 schnitzels per batch.
3. Cook the chicken for 2-3 minutes per side, flipping once, until golden brown and thoroughly cooked.
4. Replace the oil with new oil and repeat the process if the oil turns brown, which is typically caused by burnt breading pieces.
5. To drain the extra oil, place the cooked chicken between paper towels or on a wire rack.

Plate And Garnish

1. Place the chicken that has been cooked on a serving platter.
2. Parsley should be chopped finely and added on top.
3. Place the platter with the wedges.
4. Top with capers if desired.

CHICKEN FRICASSEE

Ingredients

- 2 ½ tbsp butter
- 1 onion finely diced
- ¼ cup of all-purpose flour
- 1 ½ cup of chicken broth
- ½ cup of heavy cream
- 1 pound chicken breast
- One bay leaf
- 1 cup of diced carrots
- 1 cup of sliced white mushrooms
- 1 cup of frozen peas
- 1 ½ tsp lemon juice
- salt and pepper to taste

Instructions

1. In a pot, first heat the butter over medium heat. The onion should then be sautéed until transparent.
2. Next, whisk in the flour while continuing to heat the mixture. Pour the heavy cream and chicken broth into the pot while stirring constantly until the flour is dissolved and the sauce begins to simmer.
3. The chicken breast and bay leaf can now be added. For ten minutes, everything should boil with the lid on.
4. Add the carrots, mushrooms, and peas after 10 minutes. Stir everything, then put the pot lid on. Ten minutes should be spent simmering the chicken fricassee.
5. Remove the chicken breasts and chop them into bite-sized pieces after ten minutes. After that, put them back in the pot.
6. Eliminate the bay leaf, add the lemon juice, if necessary, thin the sauce with water, and season the chicken fricassee with salt and pepper.

CHICKEN SCHNITZEL

INGREDIENTS

- 1 pound boneless skinless chicken breasts (2 large breasts)
- 1/2 cup of flour
- Two large eggs
- 1 cup of breadcrumbs, matzo meal,
- 1 tbsp paprika
- 1 tbsp sesame seeds (optional)
- 1/4 tsp salt,
- Oil with a high smoke point for frying – avocado oil preferred; grapeseed oil also works well
- Fresh lemon wedges for garnish

INSTRUCTIONS

1. Make sure every breast has a tenderloin, which is an additional piece of meat that sort of hangs off.
2. Slice the tenderloin from the breast if there is one. Trim the tenderloin and breast of any visible tendons or extra fat. Set aside the tenderloin.

3. On the cutting board, place the breast with the smooth side facing up. Find the breast's roundest thickest edge. Put your hand flat on the breast's top. Slice gently through the most comprehensive round edge of the breast, about three-quarters of the way in (dividing the top half of the breast from the bottom). Slice only halfway through.

4. The breast can be folded into two symmetrical halves, forming a "butterfly" shape. To separate the breast into two equal pieces, cut down the middle. When you're done with the pound of chicken, you ought to have four breasts that are roughly equal in size, plus possibly a few tenderloins.

5. On your kitchen countertop, spread a 2- to 3-foot-long piece of plastic wrap. Place the chicken tenderloins and breasts on the plastic, spacing them out by 2 inches. So that the meat is encased in two sheets of plastic, place another strip of plastic over the breasts.

6. Use a mallet's flat side to pound the breasts thin until they are uniformly thin throughout, about 1/8 inch thick.

7. Put all of the tenderloins and breasts that you've pounded on a dish. On your countertop, arrange three large, shallow bowls and a sizable plate that is empty. The flour should be put in the first basin. The eggs should be thoroughly combined with 2 tsp water in the second bowl. The breadcrumbs, paprika, 1/4 tsp salt, and sesame seeds (if using) should all be thoroughly combined in your third bowl. Near the area where you will place your coated schnitzels, place an empty plate.

8. A skillet or sauté pan should have around 12 inches (or more) of oil to allow for frying. Over medium heat, carefully warm the oil. Every breast should be dipped into the breading bowls one at a time while the oil is heated.

9. After that, thoroughly coat the floured breast in the egg mixture.

10. The egg-coated breast should now be placed into the breadcrumb mixture. To uniformly distribute the breadcrumbs on the breast, use a dry hand. Repeat the procedure with the remaining tenderloins and breasts.

11. Your frying oil should be hot—around 350 degrees Fahrenheit—but not smoking or sputtering hot. If you have a tenderloin on hand, you may use it to check the temperature of the oil. The coated breasts should be fried in single-layer batches until both sides are golden brown. The schnitzels should fry in the oil for around 2-3 minutes per side if the temperature is correct.

12. In a standard-sized pan, never fry more than two breasts at once; doing so will cause the oil temperature to decrease and the schnitzels to get

greasy. The schnitzels will absorb very little oil and cook up light and crisp when the oil is at the proper temperature.

13. After frying, place the schnitzels on a wire rack (or a plate or baking sheet lined with paper towels) to drain any extra oil.

14. If needed, season the schnitzels with more salt to taste. Serve hot with lemon wedges or your preferred condiment as a garnish. Both mustard and spicy sauce complement the schnitzel excellently. Take priority over who gets to eat any tenderloins you may have because they are very tender (thus the term "tenderloin"). Enjoy!

OKTOBERFEST ROAST CHICKEN 'WIESNHENDL'

INGREDIENTS

- kg (2.5 lb) whole chicken
- 3 Tbsp neutral oil
- 1 Tbsp sweet paprika powder
- 1 tsp garlic powder
- 1 tsp sea salt
- pinch of chili flakes
- black pepper

TO SERVE:

- lemon wedges
- potato salad, french fries

INSTRUCTIONS

1. **PREPARE:** The oven should be heated to 150°C/300°F/Gas 2. (Do not use fan bake or convection oven mode, it will dry out the meat). A roasting rack should be placed on a baking paper-lined oven sheet.

2. **LIFT THE BACKBONE:** Place the chicken breast on a chopping board after patting it dry with paper towels. Cut through the skin on either side of the backbone with a small, sharp knife, then cut through the bone using poultry or kitchen shears or a large, heavy knife. Throw away the spine.

3. **TIDY CHICKEN:** Flip the chicken over, then cut through the breast bone. I then chop any pieces of breast bone still attached to the chicken and toss

them aside because it is now much easier to consume. Trim the wing tips if you'd like.

4. **FORM GLAZE:** Oil, paprika, garlic powder, salt, chili flakes, and a few grinds of black pepper should all be combined. Place the chicken halves on the rack and coat the front and back of the chicken thickly and entirely with the spice mixture. Remember to check underneath the wings and drumsticks.

5. **ROTATE CHICKEN:** Roast the chicken for two hours or until it is a deep golden brown color. Use the oil spilled from the chicken after the first hour to baste the chicken occasionally. Although I think the skin is gorgeous and crispy, you can increase the oven's heat for five minutes or put it on the grill or broiler to get the skin as crisp as you like.

6. **THEN RELAX AND SERVE:** Before serving the chicken with potato salad, fries, coleslaw, and a slice of lemon, give it five to ten minutes to rest on a heated dish.

CHICKEN SCHNITZELS & GERMAN-STYLE POTATO SALAD

INGREDIENTS

For the schnitzel:

- Three chicken breasts
- Two eggs
- ½ cup of all-purpose flour
- 1 cup of breadcrumbs of choice
- Salt & pepper to taste
- Oil for frying

For the salad:

- 4-5 potatoes, roughly 1 pound or 0.5kg
- One onion yellow, white
- 3-4 pickles
- 120 ml of beef
- 1-2 tbsp of Dijon mustard
- 2 tbsp of olive oil
- 1 tbsp of white wine vinegar

- 2 tsp of sugar

INSTRUCTIONS

1. Let's create the salad first, and then we'll cook the chicken schnitzels. Take the potatoes first. Cook the potatoes in salted water for 20 minutes or until fork tender.
2. Prepare the salad dressing in the 20 minutes that remain. Chop the parsley, pickles, and onion finely. Mix this with the Dijon mustard, oil, vinegar, sugar, and broth.
3. After thoroughly combining everything, season to taste with salt and pepper.
4. Once cooked, chill the potatoes with cold water until they are lukewarm enough to handle and remove the skin.
5. Potatoes should be thinly sliced and combined with the dressing. To avoid breaking the potatoes too much, move slowly. The final potato salad should be set aside to rest.
6. I like to make chicken schnitzels big, so I'm "butterflying" the breasts. The thicker breast side should be cut through, but not completely. Open the breast, wrap it in foil or plastic wrap, then pound it evenly with a meat mallet.
7. All breasts should be well-salted and peppered on both sides.
8. Two eggs should be cracked into a bowl, beat, and then seasoned with salt and pepper.
9. Prepare the breadcrumbs and all-purpose flour, which are the remaining breading components.
10. Every piece of beef should first be floured. Finally, coat them in breadcrumbs after dipping them in the beaten eggs. When checking whether the breading is solid, apply light hand pressure.
11. Start cooking the chicken schnitzels in a pan with approximately half an inch of medium-high oil. Per side, it ought to take 5-7 minutes. Flip the food once it has turned golden brown.
12. When serving, add some chopped parsley, chives, and lemon or two slices to the schnitzels as a garnish.
13. Enjoy!

CHAPTER-5
PORK DISHES

BEST GERMAN SCHNITZEL (SCHWEINESCHNITZEL)

INGREDIENTS

- Four boneless pork steaks (to make Austrian Wienerschnitzel use thin veal cutlets)
- salt and freshly ground black pepper
- 1/2 cup of all-purpose flour combined with 1 tsp salt
- Two large eggs, lightly beaten
- 3/4 cup of plain breadcrumbs
- Oil for frying (use a neutral-tasting oil with a high smoke point)

INSTRUCTIONS

1. Use the flat side of a meat tenderizer to pound the pork chops until they are just 1/4 inch thick while sandwiched between two pieces of plastic wrap. Sprinkle a little salt and freshly ground black pepper on both sides.
2. Put the egg, breadcrumbs, and flour mixture in three shallow bowls. At every stage, coat the chops' edges and sides with flour, egg, and breadcrumbs. Be cautious not to bury the meat in the breadcrumbs. Shake off any extra crumbs gently. Schnitzel should be cooked immediately after being coated; otherwise, it won't be as crispy.
3. You don't want the Schnitzel to sit in the coating before frying, so ensure the cooking oil is hot enough at this time (about 330 degrees F). Ensure there is enough oil for the Schnitzels to "swim" in.
4. The Schnitzel should be deep-fried for 2 to 3 minutes on every side. Shortly transfer to a plate covered with paper towels.
5. Serve immediately with fresh lemon slices, parsley sprigs, or your preferred sauce. Serve with fresh leafy green salad, German potato salad, French fries, or homemade spaetzle (see recipe for homemade spaetzle).
6. Don't forget to try the much-liked Jägerschnitzel variation as well!

SCHWEINEBRATEN - GERMAN PORK ROAST

Ingredients

- 2 lb pork shoulder roast boneless, ideally with the skin
- ½ tsp caraway seeds
- One clove garlic
- ¾ tsp salt divided
- ½ tsp pepper
- 1 tsp oil
- One onion
- One carrot
- One parsnip
- 12 fl Ounces dark beer
- 1 tbsp butter
- 1 tbsp all-purpose flour

Instructions

1. 350°F/175°C oven temperature.
2. If the pork has skin, score it in a cross-shaped pattern to cut through the skin but not further into the meat. Pat the pork dry.
3. Use a pestle and mortar to grind the caraway seeds, or use a knife to cut them as finely as possible. Garlic should be grated or crushed. To make a paste, mix both ingredients with 1/2 tsp salt, pepper, and oil. Rub the paste all over the pork, getting into the skin's divots and over the exposed meat.
4. Slice the onion, carrot, and parsnip coarsely. Place the pig, skin side down, in a Dutch oven or other lidded roasting pan. Surround the pork with chopped vegetables.
5. The pork and veggies should be covered and roasted for 45 minutes after receiving most of the beer.
6. Pour the remaining beer over the pork after flipping it over so the skin side is facing up. Return to the oven and roast for another one ¼ hours, mostly uncovered, until the skin is beginning to look crisp on top and a meat thermometer registers 165°F/74°C inside.
7. The pork should be cooked through, then placed on a tray and finished under an overhead broiler or grill to crisp the skin a little more, if necessary.

The meat should then be covered to rest before carving. As the skin begins to crisp, keep an eye on it since burnt skin can happen quickly.

8. Make the gravy while the meat rests. Removing the roasting pan, strain the beer mixture. Strain the fat off the top once it has settled for a minute. Butter should be melted in a skillet before the flour is added and combined to produce a paste. Stir in the strained beet as it reduces and thickens a little.

9. Slices of pork should be served with the skin removed and with your sides and the beer gravy on top.

GERMAN PORK KNUCKLE (SCHWEINSHAXE) – SLOW-ROASTED WITH CRISPY CRACKLING!

Ingredients

- 1 x 1.25kg / 2.5lb pork knuckle
- 2 tbsp white vinegar
- Three garlic cloves, cut into 4 – 6 slivers

MARINADE RUB:

- 2 tsp salt, kosher / cooking salt, NOT table salt
- 1 tsp black pepper
- 1 tsp juniper berries
- 1 tsp caraway seeds
- 1 tsp fennel seeds

BEER GRAVY:

- 2 cups of dark German beer
- 2 cups of chicken stock/broth, low sodium
- One carrot, unpeeled, sliced 2cm / 0.8" thick
- One onion, unpeeled, halved, cut into 1.25cm / 1/2" thick slices
- One head of garlic, cut in two halves horizontally
- Five juniper berries
- Two bay leaves, preferably fresh, otherwise dried

GRAVY THICKENING AND SEASONING:

- 2 tsp cornflour/cornstarch
- 1/2 cup of water

- 1 tsp white sugar
- 1/4 – 1/2 tsp salt, kosher / cooking salt, NOT table salt

Instructions

PREPARATION AND SEASONING:

1. Prick skin: Use a small, sharp knife or even a pin (such as a safety or sewing pin) to make numerous tiny holes all over the skin of the pork knuckles. Be careful not to stab the flesh after cutting through the fat.
2. Vinegar: Do not peel back the skin; instead, brush 1 tbsp of the vinegar on the pork flesh only, getting into any crevices or cracks and the meat under the skin where it joins the flesh. Keep vinegar away from your skin.
3. With garlic, stud: With a tiny knife, make shallow slits in the pork flesh (only), then stuff with the garlic slivers.
4. Rub for seasoning: Using a mortar and pestle or a similar device, crush the materials for the rub into a coarse powder.
5. Rub olive oil on the skin of the pork after seasoning it. After that, rub the seasoning mixture all over the pork, making sure to get into all the nooks and crannies.
6. The skin on a skewer: Pulling the skin down will tighten it and prevent creases. Then, close to the base of the knuckle, thread two metal skewers through in an "X" pattern. To hold the stretched skin in place, make a small hole in the skin 2 cm / 0.8" from the base of the pig knuckle.
7. Overnight, "Marinate": Place the pork standing up on a platter, and place it in the refrigerator overnight, uncovered.

SLOW-ROASTING:

1. Set the oven to 180°C/350°F (fan 160°C).
2. Pour all the ingredients for the beer gravy into a roasting pan that is deep enough to accommodate the vegetables and liquids.
3. Put a rack above the pan by placing it there. Place the pork knuckle upright on the shelf.
4. Roast slowly for 2 hours and 10 minutes, flipping the tray halfway through. (Top with 1/2 cup of water at a time if the liquid in the pan is becoming too low and in danger of drying out.) Roast until the thickest part of the meat achieves an internal temperature of 85°C/185°F.

MAKE CRISPY PORK KNUCKLE CRACKLING!

1. The knuckle should be removed from the oven and placed on a tray.
2. Boost the oven: Oven temperature raised to 260°C/500°F (240°C fan)
3. Vinegar-brush the skin: Apply 1/2 of the vinegar from the remaining 1 tbsp to your skin. Bake for 30 minutes, flipping the tray halfway through, then basting with the remaining vinegar.
4. Crispy, dip-golden, and largely bubbling skin are ideal.
5. Before serving with German beer gravy, rest for 15 minutes.

GERMAN BEER GRAVY:

1. Pour the liquid under pressure into a saucepan after being strained. Ideally, you ought to consume 1.5 to 2 cups.
2. Simmer the liquid to thicken it. Cornflour and water should be combined, then added while stirring. To taste, add salt and sugar.
3. German beer gravy shouldn't be as thick as regular gravy; instead, it should be pretty fluid. Simmer: Simmer for 2 minutes or until it reaches a thin syrup consistency. A little water can be added if it's too thick. Too thin? Reduce the thickness by simmering. With pork knuckle, please!

GERMAN KASSELER: A CURED AND SMOKED PORK LOIN

Ingredients

- 4 liters (1 gallon) of water
- 350 grams (1-1/4 cup of) kosher salt
- 225 grams (1-1/8 cup of) sugar
- 6 grams (1 tsp) pink curing salt no.1
- One handful of fresh or dried sage leaves
- 1 tbsp juniper berries
- 1 tsp dried thyme
- 1 tsp coriander
- Garlic cloves, optional
- 1 (4- to 5-pound) pork loin without back ribs

Instructions

1. Assemble the components.

2. The brine ingredients should be combined and heated to a simmer to dissolve the salt and sugar thoroughly. Keep chilled until very cold.
3. Remove all but a thin layer of fat from the loin to prepare it. For home processing, we advise a loin roast rather than a pounds roast (back ribs attached—joint in commercial "Kasseler").
4. To submerge the loin, place it in the brine and weigh it down with a plate or other item.
5. Put in the fridge for 48 hours.
6. Pull the loin out of the brine. Throw away the brine.
7. Rinse the pork in cold water, then pat it dry. It can be dried in the fridge for up to a day without wrapping.
8. Get your smoker ready: One hour before smoking the meat, light the charcoal fire in the smoker's bottom.
9. Water should be added to 2 cups of (or so) of wood chips, ideal alder for this project.
10. Add 1/2 cup of wet wood chips to the smoking tray (or aluminum foil tray) on top of the charcoal. A foot or so above that, position the grill.
11. When the internal temperature of the beef reaches 150°F or above, place it on the grill, cover it, and let it smoke for 2 to 3 hours. As needed, add more wet chips to maintain the smoke.
12. Instead of smoking the meat, you may roast it, or if your smoker is having difficulties, just bring the heart inside and finish cooking it in the oven. The meat should be cooked for 10 minutes in the oven at 450 F. Reduce the heat to 250 F and roast the beef for 2 to 3 hours, or until it reaches 150 F.
13. Consume warm or slice and wrap. Four days in the refrigerator or 2 to 3 months in the freezer.

GERMAN WHOLE HOG (SPANFERKEL)

INGREDIENTS

For the wet rub and hog:

- 2 tbsp coarse salt (kosher)
- 2 tbsp ground ginger
- 2 tbsp curry powder
- 2 tbsp ground coriander

- 2 tbsp dried marjoram
- 2 tbsp freshly ground black pepper
- 1/2 tsp cayenne pepper
- 3/4 to 1 cup of vegetable oil
- One small pig (25 to 30 pounds), gutted and dressed

For the honey and beer glaze:

- 8 tbsp (1 stick) salted butter
- 3 tbsp minced peeled fresh ginger
- 1 cup of honey
- 1 cup of dark beer

INSTRUCTIONS

1. Mix the salt, ground ginger, curry powder, coriander, marjoram, black pepper, and cayenne pepper in a bowl and whisk in just enough oil to form a thick, flavorful paste to create the wet rub. Spread a third of the wet rub with a spatula within the pig's cavity. Cover the pig's exterior with the leftover moist rub. (If possible, marinate the pig for 12 to 24 hours in the refrigerator, covered, or in a cooler filled with ice.)
2. Make the glaze before you're prepared to spit-roast: In a large saucepan set over medium heat, melt the butter. Cook the fresh ginger for about 2 minutes or until it is aromatic but not browned. The mixture should bubble and get glazy after about two minutes of adding the beer and honey. Honey and beer glaze should be set aside. If the butter cools and solidifies, you might need to reheat the glaze.
3. It takes two people to attach the pig to the spit. Turn on the engine and spit roast the pig until the flesh is thoroughly done (an instant-read meat thermometer inserted in the deepest portion of the shoulder and ham should register 190 to 195 degrees F). After about 1-1/2 hours, begin basting the pig with the honey and beer glaze; continue basting it every 30 minutes. To keep the fire burning, add more fresh coals. Use a grill hoe or a garden hoe to the pile, rake out, or move the coals as necessary to ensure even grilling. Depending on the rotisserie, your pig, the altitude, and the weather, the cooking time will change. It usually takes 5 to 6 hours to complete.

4. Once finished, transport the pig to a stable work surface and remove the spit. Before cutting the pig, let it rest for about 20 minutes, covered loosely with aluminum foil. Any leftover honey and beer glaze should be poured over the pork.

SCHAUFELE RECIPE

Ingredients

- One pork shoulder with bones and rind
- Two onions peeled and finely chopped
- Two garlic cloves, peeled and finely chopped
- 1" fresh root ginger, grated
- 1 tsp ground cumin
- 1 cup of beer
- One can of chicken stock
- Salt and freshly ground black pepper to taste
- 1 cup of assorted veggies, shredded

Instructions

1. Use cold running water to rinse the meat, then pat it dry with paper towels.
2. Make 1 cm apart crisscross cuts on the top of the rind to create diamond-shaped patterns, then heavily salt and pepper the pork.
3. Place it on a roasting pan with its rind facing up and sprinkle ground cumin.
4. Place the shredded vegetables all around it and bake them in a previously preheated oven at 220 degrees Celsius until they are browned.
5. Pour in enough chicken broth so that the meat is covered by it by 2 cm.
6. Return the meat to the oven and continue roasting for 1-1/2 hours.
7. To keep it moist and avoid the rind turning too black, continue occasionally basting it with pan drippings.
8. Pour the beer all over the pig and place it back in the oven to glaze it for about 15 minutes before the cooking time is up.
9. The pork is ready to be served when the meat separates from the bones.
10. Lift it onto a serving platter, then drain the cooking juice into a saucepan using a fine-mesh strainer.
11. Cook for a few minutes to bring it to a slight reduction, then sprinkle it all over the pork shoulder.

12.   Serve warm with potato dumplings and a fresh salad.

SCHWENKBRATEN (GRILLED GERMAN PORK CHOPS)

INGREDIENTS

- Four bone-in pork chops

SCHWENKBRATEN MARINADE

- Two whole yellow onions (cut into thin strips)
- 1/2 cup of vegetable oil
- Four dried juniper berries (crushed)
- Four cloves garlic (roughly chopped)
- 2 tsp German-style stone ground mustard
- 2 tsp smoked paprika
- 2 tsp curry powder
- 1 tsp dried thyme
- 1 tsp dried oregano
- 1 tsp salt
- 1 tsp black pepper
- ½ tsp cayenne pepper

INSTRUCTIONS

1. In a zip-top bag, mix all marinade ingredients. To the bag, add the pork chops. Use your fingers to crush the onions while you massage the contents to coat the pork chops with the marinade equally.
2. Publish the Pork chops should be marinated for 18–24 hours.
3. For two-zone grilling (one direct heat side and one indirect heat side), preheat your grill to medium-high heat (375–425 degrees Fahrenheit). You can cook these on any grill, but cooking them over charcoal will give you a more genuine recipe.
4. Shake off any extra marinade before removing the pork chops. Do not throw away the marinade.
5. The chops should be cooked for 15-20 minutes on the indirect side of the grill to attain an internal temperature of 135 degrees F.
6. Pour the leftover marinade into a 12-inch cast iron skillet and place it on the direct side of the grill. Grill the onions until they are soft and caramelized

(you may do this while the chops are in the next step on the indirect side of the grill).

7. To finish cooking and give the chops a crisp exterior, move them to the grill's direct side. When the chops every an internal temperature of 145 degrees F, flip them every 1 to 2 minutes.
8. The pork chops should be taken off the grill and served with the caramelized marinade.

HOMEMADE BRATWURST

Ingredients

- One ¾ lb boneless pork shoulder cubed
- ¼ lb boneless beef shoulder cubed
- ½ c powdered milk
- 1 tsp salt
- 1 tsp nutmeg
- ½ tsp ground black pepper
- ½ tsp marjoram
- ¼ tsp ground mace
- ¼ tsp ground ginger
- One egg
- 1/3 c milk
- 4-5 feet hog casing for fresh sausage, rinsed

Instructions
To Make the Bratwurst

1. Utilizing a fine grinding plate in your meat grinder, grind the pork and beef cubes.
2. Mix the seasonings and powdered milk with the ground meat in a large bowl. Mix the ingredients into the meat with your hands.
3. Add the milk and egg. Using your hands, stir the ingredients until it is moistened all over.
4. Prepare your hog casings and sausage stuffer. As instructed by your sausage staffer, stuff the cases with the sausage mixture.
5. After using up all the sausage meat, form the sausage into eight links and secure the casing end.

6. Before cooking, prepared sausage can be kept in the refrigerator for up to a week.

Cooking the Bratwurst

1. You may prepare this bratwurst however you would prepare store-bought sausages: on a medium-hot grill, in a skillet, or by boiling them.
2. It is advised to cook the sausages with their links still attached. To serve, divide the sausages.

SAUMAGEN – STUFFED PIG'S STOMACH

Ingredients

- One cleaned pig's stomach
- 750 gr pork belly
- 750 gr bacon
- 750 gr potatoes
- 750 gr raw sausage meat
- Four eggs
- 2 tsp of salt
- 1 tsp of pepper
- 1 tsp of nutmeg
- 0.5 handfull of marjoram

Instructions

1. The pig's stomach should be thoroughly water-washed.
2. Potatoes, bacon, and pork belly should all be cut into small, 2 cm cubes.
3. Give the potatoes a 5-minute boil, then drain and mix them with the meats.
4. Fill the pig's stomach with the mixture, being careful not to stuff it too much as that could cause it to rip apart. Add the eggs and spices after thoroughly combining all the ingredients.
5. Tie off every one of the three openings completely to close them.
6. The stomach should now be placed in a pot of hot water and steeped for about 4 hours. It's crucial that the water not boil. The pool must be large enough to allow the stomach to float unhindered.
7. Throughout the 4 hours, rotate the stomach a few times to ensure equal cooking.

8. Remove the stomach from the water, let it drain, and then slice it into 1.5 cm thick pieces.
9. Finally, cook the slices in a pan with a little fat.
10. Sauerkraut, mashed or fried potatoes, and mustard go well with the sausage.
11. Any leftovers can be kept overnight in the refrigerator and warmed up the following day.
12. Enjoy!

GERMAN MEATBALLS

Ingredients

- 1 pound ground beef
- 1/2 pound ground pork
- 1/2 cup of finely chopped onion
- 3/4 cup of fine dry bread crumbs
- 1 tbsp snipped fresh parsley
- 1-1/2 tsp salt
- 1/8 tsp pepper
- 1 tsp Worcestershire sauce
- One large egg, beaten
- 1/2 cup of 2% milk
- 2 to 3 tbsp vegetable oil
- 1 can (27 ounces) sauerkraut, undrained
- 1/3 to 1/2 cup of water, optional
- Additional snipped parsley

Instructions

1. Mix the first ten ingredients in a bowl; form 18 meatballs, every measuring 2 inches. The meatballs are browned in a skillet with hot oil. Discard the meatballs, then drain the fat. Sauerkraut should be added to the skillet, then meatballs. Add water, cover, and boil for 15 to 20 minutes or until meatballs are thoroughly cooked. Add parsley as a garnish.

PORK SCHNITZEL RECIPE

Ingredients

- 2 lbs boneless pork chops, trimmed and sliced into 1/2" thick cutlets
- 1/3 cup of all-purpose flour
- 1 Tbsp garlic salt,
- 1/2 tsp paprika
- 1/2 tsp black pepper, freshly ground
- Three large eggs
- 2 cups of panko bread crumbs
- Olive oil, canola oil,
- Lemon wedges to serve, don't skip the lemons!

Instructions

1. Cutlets should be arranged in a single layer on a cutting board, then covered with plastic wrap to prevent splatter. Use a meat mallet or the back of a heavy saucepan to pound the cutlets until they are 1/4" to 1/8" thick.
2. Get three bowls ready. Mix 1/3 cup of flour, 1 Tbsp garlic salt, 1/2 tsp paprika, and 1/2 tsp pepper in the first. In the second, beat three eggs with a fork. Include 2 cups of panko crumbs in the third bowl.
3. Every crushed cutlet should be floured on both sides, then dipped in whisked egg, letting excess drip back into the basin before being breaded in panko crumbs. To keep your hands clean while falling, it helps to use a fork. Continue with the remaining cutlets.
4. Once every cutlet has been breaded, heat a sizable nonstick skillet over medium heat and add enough oil to coat the pan's bottom. When the oil is hot, add a few breaded cutlets and cook for 3–4 minutes on every side or until thoroughly done. If the heat is browning too soon, reduce it. Drag to a plate covered with paper towels. Juices should stream clear when one is cut open to determine its doneness. Serve with ranch dressing for kids or lemon wedges.

GERMAN PORK ROAST

Ingredients

- 3 tbsp olive oil
- Four garlic cloves minced
- 1 tsp lemon juice
- 1 tsp stone-ground mustard
- 1 tsp salt
- 1/2 tsp every dried oregano, thyme, and rosemary, crushed
- 1/4 tsp pepper
- One boneless whole pork loin roast (3 to 4 pounds)
- Four medium potatoes peeled and cut into wedges
- Three medium onions sliced into wedges
- One medium yellow tomato, cut into wedges

Instructions

1. Mix the oil, garlic, lemon juice, mustard, and seasonings in a small bowl. Rubbing the roast. Put in a small roasting pan on a rack.
2. For 20 minutes, bake uncovered at 350 degrees. Incorporate the potatoes, onions, and tomato; bake for 40–70 minutes, or until the veggies are cooked, and an instant-read thermometer registers 160°. Ten minutes should pass before slicing.

GERMAN PORK LOIN – SLOW COOKER

Ingredients

- 2-pound pork loin
- 1/4 cup of German mustard
- 1/2 tsp salt
- 1/4 tsp freshly ground pepper
- 2 tbsp cooking oil
- 1 cup of sliced onions, about one onion
- Two cloves of garlic roughly chopped
- 1/2 cup of white wine
- 2 cups of low
- 1/2 tsp dried thyme

- Two dried bay leaves
- 1/4 cup of all-purpose flour

Instructions

1. Mix the salt and pepper with the mustard. Rub the pork loin all over with this mixture.
2. An oil skillet is heating up. Add the pork loin to the skillet once it is heated but not smoking. The pork loin should be seared for three minutes on every side or until it is nicely browned.

Separate the pork.

3. The onions should soften but not brown after being added to the remaining oil for 3–4 minutes. Once the garlic is aromatic, add it and simmer for another minute.
4. White wine should be used to deglaze the pan while scraping up all the delicious brown pieces.
5. In the slow cooker insert's bottom, place the wine and onions. Place the onions on the pork loin, then cover it with chicken broth. To the liquid surrounding the roast, add the dried thyme and bay leaves.
6. Cook for 3.5–4 hours on high with the lid on.
7. The roast should be taken out and left to rest.
8. 1/4 cup of all-purpose flour and 1/4 cup of water should be combined. Mix thoroughly until the lumps are gone. To avoid lumps, stir this mixture into the liquid in the crock pot.
9. Recover the lid and simmer the mixture. Give it five minutes to steam. (If you're in a hurry, you can put the boiling liquid into a saucepan on the stove and add the flour slurry to the pot and bring it to a boil on the stovetop).
10. With the gravy, slice the pork and serve. Enjoy your Crock Pot recipe for pork roast!

CHAPTER-6
BEEF AND LAMB

OMA'S ROASTED LAMB RECIPE: LAMMBRATEN

INGREDIENTS

- 4 - 5 pounds leg of lamb
- 6 cups of buttermilk
- ½ cup of butter, room temperature
- 2 tbsp mustard
- 2 tbsp tomato paste
- 2 tbsp fresh basil and rosemary, finely chopped (if desired)
- Two cloves garlic, crushed
- 1 tsp salt
- freshly ground pepper
- 1 cup of white wine
- 1 tbsp cornstarch and a bit of cold water
- ½ cup of whipping cream

INSTRUCTIONS

1. Put the lamb roast in the buttermilk and let it marinate there for the entire night.
2. Set the oven to 350°F.
3. Rinse and dry the roast after removing it from the buttermilk. (Throw away buttermilk)
4. Create a paste by combining the butter, mustard, tomato paste, basil, rosemary, garlic, salt, and pepper. Spread all over the cooked lamb.
5. Roast for about 2 hours, or until internal temperature reaches 160°F, by placing the roast onto a rack in the roasting pan.
6. Take the roast out of the pan and let it rest, covered with foil, while you prepare the gravy.
7. Use the wine to clean out the roasting pan.
8. Gravy can be thickened by adding cornstarch dissolved in a little cold water. Stir in the whipping cream. If necessary, season with salt and pepper.

GERMAN MEATLOAF

Ingredients

- 75ml milk
- One large egg
- 40g soft white bread
- One small red onion, finely chopped
- One garlic clove, crushed
- One celery stick, finely chopped
- 50g butter
- 100g rindless bacon, chopped
- 400g beef mince
- 400g pork mince
- 1 tbsp German mustard
- Two large gherkins, chopped into pieces
- 1 tsp chopped fresh thyme
- 2 tbsp chopped fresh parsley
- Grated fresh nutmeg

INSTRUCTIONS

1. Set the oven's temperature to 180°C/fan 160°C/gas 4. In a big bowl, mix the milk and the egg. After adding, soak the bread for 15 minutes. With a fork, mash.
2. Butter should be heated slowly in a frying pan while the onion, garlic, and celery are cooked until tender. Place aside.
3. In the same pan, cook the bacon until crispy over medium heat.
4. To the bread with the herbs and spices, add the onion mixture, bacon, beef, pork, mustard, and gherkins. Blend and season. Bake for 50 minutes, or until firm, in a 900g nonstick loaf pan. Ten minutes later, stand up. Serve alongside a salad of carrots and beets.

BAUERNTOPF – GERMAN ONE-POT BEEF & PORK STEW

INGREDIENTS

- 500g ground beef
- 200g ground pork
- 600g potatoes
- Fresh crusty bread
- 1 tbsp sunflower oil
- Two yellow onions
- One red bell pepper
- One green bell pepper
- Three cloves of garlic (minced)
- One red chili (optional)
- 2 tbsp tomato purée
- 1 cup of (or 200ml) red wine
- 2 cups of (or 400ml) beef
- 1 tsp ground cumin
- 2 tsp sweet paprika powder
- 1 tbsp marjoram (dried)
- Pinch of cayenne
- Salt and pepper to taste
- Bunch of fresh parsley

INSTRUCTIONS

1. Ground beef and pork are added to a bigger saucepan with heated oil and chopped onion. Add salt and pepper to taste. On medium-high heat, cook until the food is browned (nearly no grease is left).
2. Stir in the minced garlic, tomato purée, cumin, and red paprika powder. Deglaze with a bit of red wine, then let it evaporate. Stir in the minced chili and marjoram. Cover with a lid and simmer for at least 45 minutes after adding stock. Add your chopped bell peppers after about 30 minutes, stir well, and let it boil once more. Include cubed and peeled potatoes.
3. It usually needs extra salt and black pepper, so check the seasoning. Add a dash of cayenneOnce the potatoes are cooked, take off the heat and stir in

some freshly cut parsley. Serve with some warm, crusty bread and take pleasure in.!

AUTHENTIC GERMAN GOULASH RECIPE

Ingredients

- lbs beef chuck 1 kg
- lbs onions 1 kg
- Two medium carrots
- One piece celeriac
- 2 tbsp clarified butter
- 2 tbsp tomato paste
- 1 ½ tsp sweet paprika
- 1 tsp hot paprika smoked, to taste
- 3 cups of dry red wine 750 ml,
- One ¼ cup of low sodium beef stock 300 ml
- 3-4 bay leaves
- 1 tsp dried marjoram
- ½-1 tsp caraway seeds to taste
- fine sea salt
- freshly ground black pepper

Instructions

1. Cut the meat into 1-inch (2 cm) cubes. Place aside.
2. Chop the celeriac, onions, and carrots.
3. Browned veggies In a sizable heavy-bottomed pot, warm the clarified butter. Add the vegetables and a dash of salt, and simmer for 10-15 minutes on medium heat, stirring frequently, until thoroughly golden brown. Keep them from sticking too much to the pan's bottom. If required, reduce the heat a little bit while stirring constantly.
4. To mix the tomato paste with the veggies and give it a chance to brown slightly, stir it continually for about two minutes.
5. Stir thoroughly to mix the paprika powders, both kinds.
6. Add the pepper, bay leaves, marjoram, and caraway seeds after adding the wine and stock. It all depends on the store you're using, so don't add salt just yet.

7. Simmer: Add the meat, boil, cover, and cook the beef for about two hours on low heat, stirring regularly, until it is thoroughly cooked.
8. Use salt and pepper to taste-test the food.
9. If you want the gravy to be even thicker, simmer the German goulash for 10 to 15 minutes without the lid. The sauce will be able to decrease more as a result. It's usually as thick as we prefer after the initial cooking time, so I rarely find that required.

AUTHENTIC GERMAN SAUERBRATEN RECIPE

INGREDIENTS

Marinade

- Two large yellow onions, chopped
- Two large carrots chopped
- One large leek, chopped
- Three cloves garlic, minced
- Two sprigs thyme
- Two sprigs rosemary
- Two bay leaves
- Eight juniper berries
- Six whole cloves
- Ten whole black peppercorns cracked
- 2 ½ tsp kosher salt
- 1 Tbsp sugar
- 2 cups of red wine
- 1 ½ cup of red wine vinegar
- 1 cup of beef broth
- ½ cup of golden raisins, optional

Roast

- 3-4 pounds beef chuck roast
- 2 Tbsp vegetable oil
- Ten gingersnap cookies, crushed

INSTRUCTIONS

1. Mix all marinade ingredients in a sizable oven-safe saucepan, such as a Dutch oven. Over medium-high heat, bring to a boil, cook for ten minutes, then let cool completely.
2. Place the meat into the marinade after it has cooled, then cover and chill for at least 48 hours or up to 2 weeks. To ensure that all of the meat has an opportunity to marinate fully, turn the roast every day.
3. Take the roast out of the marinade and pat it with paper towels until it is scorched. DON'T THROW AWAY THE MARINADE. To a bowl, transfer the marinade.
4. 2 tbsp of olive oil should be heated over high heat in the Dutch oven after cleaning it. Pour the marinade into the Dutch oven with the roast after searing it in the hot oil for about 2 minutes on every side.
5. When the liquids every a rolling boil, cover the pan and lower the heat to a simmer.
6. Meat should be soft after 2 to 2 ½ hours of simmering. If you'd rather, you may also place the Dutch oven in a 350°F oven with the lid on for 2 to 2 ½ hours or until the meat is fully cooked.
7. Meat should be removed from cooking liquids and left to rest for 10 minutes on a chopping board.
8. While waiting, strain the marinade, saving the liquid while throwing away the particles. Refill the Dutch oven with the fluid.
9. Crush the gingersnaps and mix them with the liquid you set aside. For 10 minutes, cook and stir over medium-low heat until the mixture thickens into a good gravy. If necessary, taste and adjust the salt and pepper.
10. Slice the sauerbraten thinly, then serve it with hot gravy.

GERMAN STYLE BEEF

Ingredients

- 2 to 3 Pounds of stew beef
- Two medium onions, chopped
- 6 to 8 strips of bacon, chopped
- 2 Tbsp butter
- Salt to taste
- Pepper to taste

- Two bay leaves
- 1-2 cups of beef stock

Instructions

1. Trim extra fat from beef before cutting it into bite-sized pieces. Melt butter in a Dutch oven or large saucepan with a cover. Stir in the bacon and onion. Let the bacon not become crunchy. With a slotted spoon, transfer the bacon-onion mixture to a colander or strainer set over a bowl. Using salt and pepper to taste, brown the steak in the pan juices. Bacon may be salty, so exercise caution when adding salt. Stir the bacon, onion, and any fluids drained in the pot. Cover the beef with stock and bay leaves. Covered, simmer the meat for 1–1/2 hours or until tender. Using roux, thicken pan juices if required.

LAMB SAUERBRATEN

Ingredients

- Red wine -- 2 cups of
- Red wine vinegar - 1-1/4 cup of
- White onion, julienne -- 3 oz
- Carrot, sliced 1/8 inch -- 1-1/2 oz
- Celery, sliced 1/8 inch on bias -- 1-1/2 oz
- Pickling spice -- 2 Tbsp.
- Lamb shanks, frenched -- 8 ea.
- Minor's Classical Reductions Reduced Brown Stock Gluten Free, prepared broth -- 2 qt.
- Oil -- 2 Tbsp.
- White onion, 3/4 inch dice -- 3 oz
- Carrot, sliced 3/4 inch -- 1-1/2 oz
- Celery, sliced 3/4 inch -- 1 oz
- Garlic, smashed -- 1 oz
- Parsley minced -- 1 Tbsp.
- Tarragon minced -- 1 Tbsp.
- Butter -- 1 Tbsp.

Instructions

1. Add red wine, vinegar, onion, carrot, celery, and pickling spice to an eight qt. Container and stir to blend. Add the lamb shanks, secure the top, and marinate for three to five days while flipping the meat daily.
2. Set the oven to 325 F.
3. Lamb should be taken out of the marinade, transferred to a parchment-lined baking sheet, and dried.
4. Oil should be added to a medium braising pan over medium-high heat, and lamb shanks should be seared for 8 to 10 minutes until golden brown on all sides. Lamb shanks should be removed and placed on a sheet pan.
5. The remaining onion, carrot, celery, and garlic should be added to the pan. Cook for 4 minutes or until the veggies are caramelized.
6. Reduce marinade by half, then strain and add to braising pan. Return the lamb shanks to the pan and cover with brown stock, about three-quarters full.
7. Place the pan in the oven with aluminum foil covering it. Lamb should be tender but not fall off the bone after two hours in the oven.
8. Lamb should be taken out of the liquid and kept aside. Reduce liquid to desired flavor profile after straining. If needed, use a cornstarch slurry to thicken the mixture. Add the shanks to the broth and garnish with butter, parsley, and tarragon.

PICHELSTEINER (BAVARIAN STEW)

INGREDIENTS

- 1 tbsp oil
- 2 pounds stewing meat (combination of beef, pork, and lamb), cubed (stewing cuts, e.g., beef chuck, pork shoulder, Boston butt)
- 2 tbsp butter
- One large yellow onion, chopped
- Three cloves garlic, minced
- One leek, chopped and thoroughly rinsed and drained in a colander
- Three large carrots peeled and cut into 1/2-inch pieces
- 1/2 small celeriac, peeled and diced (about 1-1/2 cup of)

- 6-8 medium-sized firm yellow waxy potatoes (e.g., Yukon Gold), peeled and cut into 1-inch pieces
- One small savoy cabbage, shredded (about 4 cups)
- 4 cups of chicken broth
- 1-1/2 tsp salt
- 1/2 tsp freshly ground black pepper
- 1 tsp crushed caraway seeds
- One bay leaf
- 1/4 cup of chopped fresh parsley plus more for garnish

INSTRUCTIONS

1. Working in batches to prevent crowding, heat the oil in a Dutch oven or other large, heavy pot over medium-high heat and brown the meat on all sides. Browned meat should be moved to a platter and left aside.
2. Cook the onions in the butter for 4-5 minutes or until they are tender and transparent. For one more minute, add the garlic. Leeks should be added and cooked for 4-5 minutes until tender. Cook the carrots and celeriac for a further 4-5 minutes after adding them. The remaining ingredients, minus the parsley, should be added to the saucepan with the meat. The pot is covered.
3. If using a stovetop, stew the meat at a low temperature for 60 to 90 minutes, depending on how tender you want. Add salt and pepper to taste before incorporating the parsley. Throw away the bay leaf.
4. If using a Dutch oven or another oven-safe vessel for conventional oven cooking: Set the oven's temperature to 325 F. Place the Dutch oven on the center rack and bake for 90–120 minutes or until the meat is incredibly soft (add more liquid if necessary), without stirring. Add salt and pepper to taste before incorporating the parsley. Throw away the bay leaf.
5. Serve with some parsley on top. Serve with a fresh salad or some crusty bread.
6. Because it tastes even better the next day, pichelsteiner is a fantastic recipe to prepare ahead of time.

GRANDMA'S LAMB SHANKS IN A WINE SAUCE

INGREDIENTS

- Four lamb shanks
- 1 cup of shallots
- Two cloves garlic
- 2 cups of celery
- 1½ cups of carrots
- 2 tbsp oil
- Four twigs rosemary
- Three bay leaves
- One handful parsley
- 2 tbsp raisins or sultanas
- 1 cup of red wine fruity
- 1 cup of lamb stock
- One ⅔ cup of whipped cream
- 2 tbsp butter
- Salt and pepper to taste

INSTRUCTIONS

1. Top and bottom heat should be used to pre-heat the oven to 320°F (160°C); convection is not recommended.
2. The lamb shanks should be rinsed under running water, any extra tendons cut off and then patted dry with paper towels. Add salt and pepper to the rub.
3. The garlic and shallots should be peeled. Slice the garlic and finely dice the shallot. Cut the carrots and celery roots into little cubes after cleaning and peeling them. Slice the rosemary needles finely after removing them from the branches in the opposite direction of their growth.
4. Lamb shanks are browned in a casserole dish with hot oil or butter. They ought to smell good when roasting. From the casserole dish, could you take out the shanks and set them aside?
5. The shallots should first be added to the hot casserole dish and lightly fried. Add the celery root and garlic after three minutes, and sauté them both

briefly as well. Bay leaves, rosemary, and raisins should be added to the casserole dish and shanks. Mix everything with the lamb stock and red wine.

6. The lamb shanks should simmer for 2.5 hours in the oven once the casserole dish has been covered with a lid.

7. Several times, baste the shanks with the braising liquid. After the braising period, please take off the top and let them roast for an additional 30 minutes.

8. The shanks should be removed from the casserole, covered with foil to keep warm, and left aside.

9. Pour the casserole dish's braising liquid into a pot.

10. After adding the cream, allow the stock to boil briefly. Salt and pepper are used to season the red wine sauce properly. Add the butter at this point to thicken the sauce.

11. Place the lamb shanks on a dish and top with the red wine sauce, or serve it alongside. Sprinkle the lamb shanks with the parsley that has been finely chopped.

CLASSIC, SAVORY SHEPHERD'S PIE (WITH BEEF AND LAMB)

Ingredients

For the Mashed Potatoes:

- 3-1/2 pounds (1.6kg) russet potatoes (about four prominent), peeled and cut into 1-inch pieces
- Kosher salt
- 6 tbsp (85g) unsalted butter, cubed

For the Meat Sauce:

- 1-1/2 cup of (360ml) homemade or store-bought low-sodium chicken stock
- Two packets of unflavored gelatin (about 5 tsp s; 1/2 ounce; 14g)
- 2 tbsp (30ml) vegetable oil
- 2-1/2 pounds (1kg) of ground beef or lamb,
- One large yellow onion (about 14 ounces; 400g), diced
- Three medium carrots (about 8 ounces; 225g), diced
- Two ribs of celery (about 4 ounces; 110g), diced
- 2 medium cloves garlic, minced
- 2 tbsp (30ml) tomato paste

- 1 cup of (240ml) dry red wine
- Two sprigs thyme
- One bay leaf
- 1 tbsp (15ml) Worcestershire sauce
- 1 tsp (5ml) Marmite (optional)
- 2 tbsp (15g) all-purpose flour
- 8 ounces (225g) frozen peas
- Kosher salt and freshly ground black pepper

To Assemble:

- 1-1/2 cups of (360ml) heavy cream
- Grated Parmigiano-Reggiano cheese for topping (optional)

Instructions

1. Cubed potatoes should be placed in a colander and rinsed in cold water until the water is clear for the mashed potatoes. Place in a sizable saucepan and cover with at least 2 inches of cold water. Water should be salted to a point where it resembles the sea. Water should be heated to a rolling boil over high heat, then lowered to a simmer for 10 to 15 minutes or until a knife pierces the potatoes easily. Potatoes should be drained in a colander before being given a 30-second hot water rinse. Place potatoes in a big bowl.
2. Mash potatoes with butter using a potato masher, food mill, or ricer. To stop a skin from forming, smooth the surface and then press plastic wrap against it. Save until you're ready to put it together.
3. For the Meat Sauce, in the meantime: Gelatin should be sprinkled over the stock in a 2-cup of liquid measuring cups before being set aside.
4. In a big Dutch oven, heat the oil until it shimmers. Use a potato masher or a large whisk to break up the meat while it cooks. Add half of the ground meat and simmer, stirring and scraping the bottom of the saucepan, until nicely browned, 6 to 8 minutes. Reduce heat as required to prevent burning. Add remaining meat and simmer, breaking it up with a masher or whisk, until reduced to tiny bits, about 3 minutes. Use a metal spoon to remove the majority of the rendered fat from the meat if there is an excessive amount, leaving only a few tbsp in the pot. For about 4 minutes, sauté the onion, carrots, celery, and garlic while swirling and scraping the bottom of the pan.

5. Cook the tomato paste for one minute while stirring over medium heat. Over high heat, add red wine and bring to a simmer. Cook, stirring occasionally, until almost all of the liquid has evaporated. Add the Worcestershire sauce, Marmite, thyme, bay leaf, and any leftover chicken stock. Add flour to the pot of ground beef and stir. Bring to a simmer, lower heat to medium, and simmer for about 20 minutes or until sauce is reduced and thick. Throw away the bay leaf and thyme sprigs. Peas are added after seasoning with salt and pepper.

6. To Put Together and Bake: Pre-heat the oven to 425°F (220°C) and center the oven rack. The cream should be boiled in a big pan before assembly. Add the potatoes and gently mix everything. Add salt and pepper to taste. The potatoes can now be assembled.

7. On a rimmed baking sheet lined with foil, place a nine-by-13-inch baking dish. Be careful not to add more meat sauce than is necessary. (Depending on the precise dimensions of your baking dish, you might not need the entire amount of spice.) Add mashed potatoes on top, spreading them out with a spatula to completely cover the surface. Create a dotted pattern on the potatoes' surface using a spatula. Suppose using, top with grated Parmesan cheese.

8. Place in oven, and bake for 20 minutes, or until the top is browned and the dish is thoroughly heated. During the final few minutes of cooking, place the casserole on a rack approximately 6 inches under a hot broiler for a deeper browning. (Oversee the potatoes to avoid scorching them.)

9. Before serving, let stand for 15 to 20 minutes. The casserole can be put together, wrapped in plastic, and kept in the fridge for up to two days. For around 35 minutes, reheat the food at 350°F (180°C), then brown the top under the broiler.

BEST FRIKADELLEN- GERMAN MEATNALLS

INGREDIENTS

- 250 g minced /ground pork 0.5 lb - you could replace with beef mince if you like
- 250 g minced / ground beef 0.5 lb
- One white, stale, dry crusty roll close or dry (about 100 g or 3.5 oz) of white bread is good,

- One egg medium size
- One onion around 70 g or 2.4 oz
- 1 tbsp vegetable or sunflower oil for frying the onions
- 1 tsp mustard
- 1 tsp salt
- ½ tsp black pepper
- 1 tsp ground sweet paprika
- 1 tsp dried marjoram if not available, use sage
- 1 tsp dried parsley can be substituted with fresh parsley
- butter, clarified butter, or vegetable oil for frying the meatballs

INSTRUCTIONS

1. The bread rolled in water for a while. With your hands, a spoon, and a sieve, squeeze out any residual liquid until it has become soft. This is crucial because if the mixture gets too wet, the meatballs' texture will be affected.
2. Slice the onion extremely thinly after peeling. Fry in oil in a frying pan until it begins to brown.
3. Now place the ground beef in a sizable basin. Add the bread pulp, onion, egg, mustard, salt, pepper, marjoram, parsley, and paprika. Stir everything together with a wooden spoon or your hands until it is thoroughly combined.
4. To see if the seasoning is correct, form a handful of the mixture into a ball and fry it in oil.
5. With your hands, shape tiny meatballs. Depending on your preferences, the size. To portion them, I like to use an ice cream scoop because evenly proportioned frikadellen will aid in even cooking. Mine had a diameter of around 5 cm and weighed about 50 gr/1.7 Ounces each.
6. A big frying pan should have enough oil or clarified butter to cover the bottom. On medium heat, cook the meatballs for about 5-7 minutes on every side. Avoid turning the meatballs too soon; instead, let them fry for a little longer to develop a firmer consistency. They might disintegrate otherwise upon turning. Ensure the oil is not too hot since this will cause the outside to crisp up too rapidly and the inside to remain raw.
7. Before serving, place on a paper towel to absorb any extra fat.
8. Eaten either warm or cold.

9. Making it in an oven
10. Place the meatballs on a baking sheet covered with parchment paper and preheat the oven to 200°C/ 392°F. Depending on size, bake them in the oven for 30 to 40 minutes.

GERMAN MEATBALLS IN WHITE SAUCE (KÖNIGSBERGER KLOPSE)

Ingredients
For the Meatballs:

- Two slices of day-old bread
- 1 tbsp unsalted butter
- Two small onions, one chopped finely, one quartered
- 1/2 pound ground pork
- 1/2 pound ground beef
- 1 to 2 large egg yolks
- 1/2 tsp salt
- 1/4 tsp freshly ground black pepper
- 4 cups of vegetable broth
- Five whole black peppercorns cracked
- Four juniper berries, cracked, optional
- One bay leaf, optional

For the Sauce:

- 2 tbsp unsalted butter
- 2 tbsp all-purpose flour
- 24 capers, drained
- 2 to 4 ounces of white wine
- 1 to 2 tbsp lemon juice
- 2 to 4 tbsp sour cream
- One pinch of sugar, optional

Instructions
Make the Meatballs

1. Assemble the components.

2. The day-old bread should be soaked in water and squeezed until nearly dry. Cut it into little pieces.
3. When the onion is transparent, sauté it in melted butter. Cool a little.
4. Put the beef and pork, sautéed onions, and bread chunks in a big basin.
5. One egg yolk, salt, and pepper should all be added.
6. Add a few tbsp of broth if the mixture cannot be shaped into meatballs. Twelve meatballs should be formed.
7. Add the remaining broth, quartered onion, cracked peppercorns, cracked juniper berries, and bay leaf (if using) to a large pot. Bring to a gentle boil.
8. Carefully include the meatballs. Cook for 12 minutes or until done. Keep the meatballs warm after removal. To measure the liquid, strain it into a cup.

Make the Sauce

1. Assemble the components.
2. Make a roux by melting the butter in a pan and stirring in the flour.
3. As you whisk to keep the sauce smooth, slowly incorporate 1-1/2 cup of s of the drained meatball cooking liquid into the roux.
4. White wine and capers should be added. Sour cream, lemon juice, and a sprinkle of sugar, if used, can be added to season the sauce.
5. To further bind the sauce, if desired, add the second egg yolk. After adding, warm the sauce; do not boil as this may cause the egg yolk to curdle. The curdled egg won't change the taste; it just doesn't look good.
6. Warm the sauce up before adding the meatballs and serving.
7. Enjoy.

CHAPTER-7
SEAFOOD

GERMAN FISH BALLS WITH GREEN SAUCE

Ingredients
Fish meatballs

- 500 fish fillets, such as trout
- 2eggs, lightly beaten
- Two tsp salt
- ½ cup of plain breadcrumbs
- Two tsp finely chopped fresh dill
- Two tsp finely chopped fresh parsley

Green sauce

- 60 unsalted butter
- One large French shallot, finely chopped
- 250 ml(1 cup of) fish stock
- Two tbsp finely chopped spinach, amaranth,
- ¼ cup of chopped sorrel (optional)
- ¼ cup of finely chopped parsley
- Two tbsp chopped dill
- Two tbsp finely chopped garlic chives
- 1sage leaf, finely chopped
- salt and black pepper to season
- ½ cup of sour cream at room temperature

Instructions

1. To prepare the meatballs, pulse the fish in a food processor, crush it in a meat grinder, or finely slice it with a knife. Simply mix every ingredient in a bowl and shape the mixture into meatballs approximately the size of a walnut. The fish balls should be cooked by slowly lowering them into a large pot of boiling, salty water one at a time; they will float. Reduce the heat to a barely simmer because letting it boil again would cause your fish balls to disintegrate. Until the meatballs float, gently simmer. Expect the cooking to

take around 10 minutes in total. The fish balls should be removed from the hot water and put aside.

2. Make the green sauce in the interim. In a big frying pan over medium-high heat, melt the butter. When it's hot, add the shallot and cook, stirring, for about 3 minutes, until it's translucent and soft (avoid letting them brown). Bring to a boil after adding the stock. The sauce should reduce by roughly one-third after several minutes of vigorous boiling. Stir in all the herbs while lowering the heat as far as it will go. Let them all fade up. Turn off the heat after seasoning with salt and black pepper to taste.

3. When all the fish balls are prepared, reheat the sauce to a warm temperature and brush it on the fish balls. When the sauce bubbles up again, remove it from the heat; please wait for it to stop, then gradually whisk in the sour cream. Serve right away after making one more salt and black pepper adjustment.

GERMAN BAKED COD IN MUSTARD CREAM

INGREDIENTS

- 1 ½ lb cod filets
- kosher salt
- fresh cracked pepper. I prefer mixed peppercorns for this
- ½ cup of heavy cream
- 2 Tbs quality whole grain mustard
- fresh dill leaves

INSTRUCTIONS

1. 350°F oven temperature.
2. In a 13 x 9 baking dish, place the fish. Add salt and pepper to taste (at least 1/4 t salt). Separately, mix the Dijon and cream. Add to the fish. Add some tiny, torn dill leaves on top of the fish.
3. Fish should flake readily with a fork after 15 minutes of baking at 350F. Four servings.

FISCHBRÖTCHEN

Ingredients

- Two eggs
- Four cornichon pickles
- 1/2 apple, not too sweet
- 2 tbsp mayo
- 1/2 cup of whole milk Greek yogurt
- 1 tbsp pickle juice
- 1 tsp fresh lemon juice
- 1/4 cup of fresh parsley, chopped
- 2 tbsp milk
- 1/3 cup of flour
- 1/3 cup of breadcrumbs
- Two fillets of Pacific cod are Available in Our Seafood Subscription Box
- 2-1/2 tbsp butter
- Two brioche rolls
- Two large leaves of butter lettuce

Instructions

MAKE REMOULADE

1. One egg should be boiled for 10 to 12 minutes until complex, then peeled under cold water. Mix cornichons with fine dice. Apple should be cored and diced finely. Mix the mayo, yogurt, pickle juice, and lemon juice. Add salt and pepper to taste. Add parsley and stir.

COOK FISH

1. The second egg should be beaten with milk and a dash of salt before being transferred to a shallow basin or plate. Place breadcrumbs and flour on two different scales. The order of coating the fish in flour, egg mixture, and lastly, breadcrumbs.
2. In a skillet over medium heat, melt the butter. Fish should be cooked for 4 to 5 minutes per side. Transfer to a fresh plate that has been paper towel lined.

BUILD SANDWICHES

1. Brioche should be lightly toasted in a skillet or toaster. Mix lettuce, fish, and remoulade to make sandwiches. On the side, dispense the remaining remoulade sauce.

GERMAN BRAT SEAFOOD BOIL

Ingredients

- One package (19 ounces) of uncooked bratwurst links
- One medium onion, quartered
- Two bottles (12 ounces each) of beer or 3 cups of reduced-sodium chicken broth
- 1/2 cup of seafood seasoning
- Five medium ears of sweet corn cut into 2-inch pieces
- 2 pounds small red potatoes
- One medium lemon, halved
- 1 pound cod fillet, cut into 1-inch pieces
- Coarsely ground pepper

Instructions

1. Bratwurst should be grilled covered over medium heat, often rotating, for 15-20 minutes or until the flesh is no longer pink. Covered, grill onion for 3–4 minutes on every side or until lightly browned. Grilled bratwurst should be cut into 2-inch pieces.
2. Corn, potatoes, lemon, bratwurst, and onion are added to a stockpot with two qt. Of water, beer, and seafood seasoning. Up to a boil. Reduce heat; cover and simmer for 15-20 minutes or until potatoes are cooked. Cod is added and cooked for 4-6 minutes or until it flakes easily with a fork. Transfer to a big serving bowl after draining. Add some black pepper.

BIER FISCH (GERMAN BEER FISH)

Ingredients

- 3 pounds fish, whole carp
- two to three pounds whole fish with head, dressed
- 2 tbsp butter

- One every onion chopped
- One every celery stalk chopped
- ½ tsp salt
- Six every peppercorn
- Three every clove, whole
- Four slices lemon
- One every bay leaves
- 10 ounces beer, one bottle
- Six every gingersnap cookie crushed
- 1 tbsp sugar
- One parsley leaves
- for garnish, fresh

Instructions

1. In Germany, this dish has a long history of use. The sauce has sour, spiciness, and sweetness to it. Fresh carp is used in Germany. However, other fish may be used in its place because it is difficult to find.
2. Fish heads should be removed and saved to make fish stock for other dishes. Fish should be laid out as flatly as possible with the backbones broken. In a skillet, melt the butter. Mix in the onion, celery, salt, pepper, and cloves. Add a bay leaf and lemon slices on top.
3. Put the fish there. Booze it up. Fish should barely flake with a fork after 15 to 20 minutes of simmering undercover. Fish should be moved to a dish and kept warm with foil.
4. Using a strainer, push some of the vegetables through the cooking liquid. Stir 1½ cups of filtered liquid into the skillet with the gingersnaps and sugar. Cook while constantly stirring until thickened. Use parsley as a fish garnish. Pass the side dish of boiled potatoes and the sauce to drizzle over the fish.

FISCHBRÖTCHEN: GERMAN COD SANDWICHES

INGREDIENTS

- Two eggs
- Four cornichon pickles
- ½ apple, not too sweet

- 2 tbsp mayo
- 100 g whole milk Greek yogurt
- 1 tbsp pickle juice
- 1 tsp fresh lemon juice
- ¼ c chopped fresh parsley
- 2 tbsp milk
- 40 g flour
- 40 g breadcrumbs
- Two cod fillets
- 40 g butter
- Two great brioche rolls are my Weizenbrötchen if you have time to make them!
- Two large leaves of butter lettuce

INSTRUCTIONS

1. One egg should be hardboiled before being peeled and placed in cold water. Using four little cornichons, finely dice the food. Chop the apple in half and remove the core. Mix the mayo, yogurt, pickle juice, and lemon juice. Add salt and pepper to taste. Add chopped parsley after stirring.

2. Transferring the egg to a wide plate or shallow basin after whisking it with some milk and salt. Place some breadcrumbs and flour on two different scales. Fish is first dusted with flour, then covered with egg mixture, and finally, breadcrumbs. Cook the fish for 4 to 5 minutes on every side in melted butter over medium heat. Transfer to a dry plate that is paper towel-covered.

3. Rolls should be cut in half and lightly toasted in a skillet or toaster. Place some lettuce on the bottom of the registration, followed by the fish and remoulade sauce. Top the sandwich off with the remaining roll half. On the side, dispense the remaining remoulade sauce.

SAILOR'S SWEETHEART

INGREDIENTS

- 2 pounds pollock filets alternatively Swai, Tilapia
- 2 pounds carrots
- One large onion

- 1 tbsp. garlic paste
- 2 tbsp. Butterschmalz (clarified butter)
- 1 cup of chicken broth
- ½ bunch of dill
- 1 cup of sour cream
- 2 tbsp. mustard
- 1 ½ tbsp. honey
- Salt and pepper to taste

INSTRUCTIONS

1. Turn the oven on to 375 degrees Fahrenheit.
2. Sliced carrots that have been peeled.
3. Melt oil or butterscotch over medium heat.
4. Lightly braise the carrots, onions, garlic paste, and honey.
5. Add chicken broth to the deglazing process, boil for 3–4 minutes, and then set away.
6. Finely chop the dill.
7. Sour cream, mustard, and dill are combined in a small bowl and added to the carrots.
8. Tap water should be used to rinse and dry the fish filets.
9. Place in a casserole pan after seasoning with salt and pepper.
10. Bake for 20 to 25 minutes, then cover with the carrot mixture.

FISH CAKES WITH HERBED SAUCE (GERMAN)

INGREDIENTS
FOR FISH CAKES

- 2potatoes (peeled)
- 1onion divided per Prep
- 9ounces white fish fillets (skinned & bones removed)
- 9ounces smoked fish fillets (skinned & bones removed, may use shrimp as I did & see Note below)
- flour (sml amt for dusting)
- canola oil (for shallow frying)
- salt & freshly ground black pepper

FOR HERBED SAUCE

- 2ounces mixed herbs (See note Re Herb Mix)
- 4tbsp Quark (or sub cream cheese)
- 2tbsp milk
- 2tbsp mayonnaise
- 2tsp mustard (sweet variety)
- 1tsp lemon juice
- 2eggs (hard-boiled & roughly chopped)

Instructions

1. Grate potatoes coarsely and squeeze out any extra liquid. Grate the onion finely. To the potatoes, add half of the onion; save the other half for the sauce.
2. Fish fillets should be roughly chopped, added to a food processor with some freshly ground black pepper, and blended to a smooth paste.
3. Mix the potato/onion mixture with the fish paste and season to taste with salt, keeping in mind that the smoked fish already contains some salt. Cut a cross into eight rounds and set aside.
4. Clean the food processor, then make the sauce by pulsing your preferred herbs until they are finely chopped (see the remark about the herb mix below).
5. To make a slightly chunky purée that still has some texture, add the other sauce components and the saved shredded onion. Taste the sauce, season with salt and pepper to taste, then transfer to a bowl and reserve.
6. Fish cakes are delicately dusted in flour. Fry cakes (in 2 batches as necessary) for about 3 minutes on every side in oil, heated to a depth of 1/2 inch over medium heat. Reheat the oil and drain on paper towels before cooking the second batch. Serve a fresh tomato salad and fish cakes with sauce.
7. Choose among parsley, chives, chervil, dill, marjoram, sorrel, coriander, basil, tarragon, borage, lovage, rocket, or baby spinach for your herb mixture, according to the recipe. Sparingly use the more potent herbs.
8. NOTE (Added 4/3/08): I suddenly ran out of smoked fish when I cooked this recipe, so I substituted tiny Icelandic shrimp, which worked well. I suggest

adding 1 tsp (or more as desired) of Old Bay Seasoning to the fish cake mixture if you prepare the dish with this substitute.

BREMER- GERMAN FISH SANDWICH (FISCHBRÖTCHEN)

INGREDIENTS

- Four cod fish cakes.
- Four pickled gherkins
- Four crusty white rolls
- Four large leaves of salad
- 4 tbsp remoulade (alternativley Tartar Sauce)
- 4 tbsp tomato ketchup
- 4 tbsp roasted onions

INSTRUCTIONS

1. Make thin slices of cornichons.
2. The bread roll should be cut in half horizontally.
3. One of the bread roll slices should have 1 tbsp of remoulade. Place the fishcakes, lettuce, and cornichons on top. Before sealing the sandwich, spread ketchup on the other half of the bread roll and add roasted onions.
4. The German fish sandwich may be served with fries, fried potatoes, or a green salad.

GERMAN FISH MEATBALLS WITH GREEN SAUCE

INGREDIENTS

FISH BALLS

- 1-pound groundfish
- Two eggs, lightly beaten
- 2 tsp salt
- 6 tbsp plain breadcrumbs
- 2 tsp minced fresh dill
- 2 tsp minced fresh parsley

GREEN SAUCE

- 1/4 cup of unsalted butter

- One large shallot, about 1/3 cup of minced
- 1 cup of fish stock
- 2 tbsp minced spinach, amaranth
- 1/4 cup of chopped sorrel, optional
- 1/4 cup of minced parsley
- 2 tbsp chopped dill
- 2 tbsp minced garlic chives
- One sage leaf minced
- Salt and black pepper
- 1/2 cup of sour cream at room temperature

INSTRUCTIONS

1. Simply mix all the ingredients in a bowl and shape the mixture into small meatballs—about the size of a walnut—to make the meatballs. To cook, gently lower the fish balls one at a time into a large saucepan of boiling, salted water. They'll go under. Reduce the heat to a simmer; if you let it burn again, the fish balls may be ruined. Until the meatballs float, gently simmer. Expect the cooking to take around 10 minutes in total.
2. The fish balls should be removed from the hot water and put aside.
3. Make the green sauce while the poaching water is heating. In a sizable saute pan set over medium-high heat, melt the butter. When it's hot, add the shallot and cook for 3 minutes or until it's translucent and soft. Keep them from browning. Bring to a boil after adding the stock. The sauce should reduce by roughly one-third after several minutes of vigorous boiling.
4. Stir in all the herbs while lowering the heat as far as it will go. Let them all fade up. Turn off the heat after seasoning with salt and black pepper to taste.
5. Re-heat the sauce to a warm temperature and then pour it over the fish balls once they are all cooked. When the sauce bubbles up again, remove it from the heat; please wait for it to stop, then gradually whisk in the sour cream. Serve right away after making one more salt and black pepper adjustment.

FISH CAKES WITH CUCUMBER YOGURT ('FISCHKÜCHLE MIT GURKENJOGHURT')

Ingredients
For the cucumber yogurt:

- 1 European cucumber, finely shredded
- 1/4 tsp salt
- 1/2 tsp sugar
- 12 ounces (340 g) regular full-fat (3.8 or 10 % fat content)
- 1 tsp white wine vinegar
- 1/2 tbsp olive oil
- 1 tbsp chopped mint leaves

For the fish cakes:

- 1/3 cup of whole milk, heated just below a light simmer
- One white bread roll cut into small cubes
- 1 pound (450 g) cod fillet, chopped into a rough paste (you can do it by hand or use your food processor)
- 1 tsp finely chopped capers
- 1/2 tsp Dijon mustard
- 1 tbsp chopped dill leaves
- 1/3 tsp ground coriander seeds
- 1/3 tsp ground white pepper
- 1/3 tsp ground cumin
- 1/2 tsp sugar
- One egg,
- salt, to taste
- 1-2 tbsp breadcrumbs
- clarified butter for frying

Instructions
Prepare the cucumber yogurt:

1. Cucumber shreds are mixed with salt and sugar, then let for 10 minutes to marinate. Squeeze out any extra moisture after wrapping the cucumber

shreds in a kitchen towel or cheesecloth. Because they would otherwise dilute the yogurt, the cucumber shreds must be extremely dry.

2. Whisk the yogurt, cucumber, vinegar, olive oil, and mint leaves in a bowl. To taste, increase the vinegar and salt. At least 30 minutes should pass before serving the cucumber yogurt once it has been covered and chilled.

Prepare the fish cakes:

1. Bread roll cubes should soak in the heated milk for at least 10 minutes after being added.

2. Cod that has been cut, bread roll cubes that have been soaked, capers, mustard, dill leaves, coriander seeds, white pepper, cumin, sugar, and egg should all be combined in a big mixing bowl. Mix briefly, then add salt to taste. To bind the batter, add 1-2 tbsp of breadcrumbs. When shaped into a patty, it ought to retain its shape while being incredibly soft. Using your preferred size, shape the batter into individual fish cakes.

3. A sizable nonstick saute pan is heated over medium heat with lots of clarified butter. To prevent your fish cakes from burning, the fat must completely cover the pan surface and be at least 1/4 inch high. Put as many fish cakes as possible in the pan and fry for 3 to 4 minutes or until golden brown on the first side. Turn them over carefully, then fry the other side until both are entirely done and golden brown. Fry fish cakes until all the batter has been used up, then place them on paper towels to drain.

GERMAN PLUM DUMPLINGS (ZWETSCHGENKNOEDEL)

Ingredients

- 1 cup of quark,
- 10 tbsp butter, divided
- 3 tbsp sugar
- 1 tsp lemon zest
- One large egg
- 3/4 cup of all-purpose flour
- 1/4 tsp baking powder
- Dash kosher salt
- 12 plums
- 12 sugar cubes

- 4 to 5 pieces Zwieback, crushed
- 1/2 cup of cinnamon sugar

Instructions

1. Assemble the components.
2. From quark or yogurt cheese, drain any liquids, then pat the surface dry.
3. 7 tbsp softened butter, sugar, and quark should be thoroughly combined. Lemon zest and egg are united.
4. Salt, baking powder, and flour should be incorporated or sifted. Blend into the batter to create a soft, supple dough.
5. For about an hour, refrigerate the dough.
6. Until the water in a large pan of salted water boils, reduce the heat.
7. To remove the pit, wash the plums and cut them in half (along the "seam" is ideal). Put a sugar cube in its place, then press the sliced edges together.
8. Form a ball with floured hands using about 1/12th of the dough, and then press the ball flat on a lightly dusted surface. A plum is wrapped in dough, which is then tightly compressed.
9. Depending on size, simmer plums in boiling water for 15 to 25 minutes or until tender. Testing one or user experience is the only way to know if they are finished. The water shouldn't boil because doing so causes the dough to crumble.
10. Melt the remaining butter in a pan and add the bread crumbs or Zwieback while boiling. Toast and warm the crumbs.
11. Drain the dumplings well after removal. Serve with cinnamon and sugar or dusted with powdered sugar after rolling in buttery crumbs. They could also be served with whipped cream or vanilla sauce.

GERMAN BIENENSTICH (BEE STING CAKE)

Ingredients

Cake

- 1-1/2 – 1-3/4 cup of [210-230g] flour (all-purpose, see note below)
- 2 TBSP [30g] sugar
- 2 tsp [1/4 Ounces / 7g] yeast (fast-rising)
- pinch of salt
- One egg

- 1/4 cup of [57g] butter (melted)
- 1/3 cup of [75ml] milk

Topping

- 1/2 cup of [113g] butter
- 1 TBSP honey
- 5-6 TBSP sugar
- 1-1/2 TBSP heavy whipping cream
- 1 TBSP vanilla sugar
- 3/4 cup of [80g] sliced almonds

Filling

- 2 cups of [400ml] heavy whipping cream
- 3 Tbsp vanilla pudding powder
- 1 tsp vanilla sugar

Instructions

1. In a medium-sized mixing basin, stir the flour, sugar, yeast, and salt. Add milk, egg, and melted butter. To make a soft dough into a ball, mix ingredients with a wooden spoon. If the dough is sticky, add more flour until your fingers can handle it without sticking.
2. In the bowl, knead the dough 5–7 times or until it appears and feels smooth.
3. Allow the dough to rest for 30 minutes while it is towel-covered.
4. Heat the oven to 350°F (176°C).
5. Melt butter, honey, sugar, and vanilla sugar in a pot over medium-low heat to produce the honey almond topping. Add the cream when the butter has melted, and stir again until the sugar is dissolved.
6. When ready to add the almond slices and vanilla extract—if you're not using vanilla sugar—remove the skillet from the heat. The topping should be kept warm until it is time to use it.
7. An 8x8 inch (20x20 centimeter) baking pan should be lined with parchment paper so the edges dangle over the sides. After pressing the dough onto the pan, poke it several times with a fork.

8. Spread the topping evenly over the dough after pouring it on. Bake for approximately 30 minutes (check at 25 minutes and bake for 5–7 minutes if necessary). When finished, the topping will be golden brown.
9. For a few minutes, let the cake cool in the pan. Transfer the cake to a wire rack by grabbing the parchment paper's edges. Give the cake 10 to 20 minutes to cool.
10. Use a long serrated knife to slice the cake lengthwise into two thin slices once you can touch it easily with your fingertips (see photographs above).
11. Use the same serrated knife to cut the top layer (the one with the topping) into nine pieces after transferring it to a cutting board. If you wait until the cake has chilled, you risk cutting it and pushing the filling out the sides. It is MUCH easier to cut this top layer while the cake is still warm rather than when you're ready to serve it. Let the components for the bottom and top layers cool.
12. Make the filling while the cake is cooling. Heavy cream should be poured into a medium mixing basin. Beat to soft peaks before adding the pudding powder and vanilla sugar (or extract). If desired, add more pudding powder or vanilla after tasting the filling.
13. Put the plate with the bottom cake layer on it. Using a palette knife, spread the filling over the bottom cake layer. Then, piece by piece gently arranges the nine parts of the top layer of the cream filling. The cake should be covered or wrapped in plastic and chilled for an hour or until the filling is set.
14. Allow the cake to warm up for a few minutes before cutting and serving it when ready. When cutting the bottom layer, be careful not to press down too firmly on the top layer because this will cause the filling to leak out.
15. The day you create the cake is the ideal day to consume it.

BLUSHING MAID - GERMAN RASPBERRY DESSERT

INGREDIENTS

- 10ounces raspberries, frozen
- 3slices pumpernickel bread
- 2ounces dark chocolate, chopped

- 2tbsp Chambord raspberry liquor,
- 2tbsp cherry juice
- 1/2cup of whipping cream
- 10ounces yogurt, plain
- 2tbsp sugar
- 1tbsp vanilla

Instructions

1. The raspberries should only slightly thaw (they shouldn't get too soft!).
2. Pumpernickel or bread is processed into coarse crumbs, combined with chopped chocolate, and placed in a glass dish with juice or schnaps.
3. The cream should be stiffened.
4. Yogurt is blended with sugar, vanilla, and vanilla sugar.
5. Add whipped cream and fold.
6. Over the soggy bread crumbs, pour yogurt cream.
7. Place raspberries on top and chill for about an hour (it tastes better if it's somewhat sopped through).

STRAWBERRY RHUBARB TRIFLE

Ingredients

- 1 lb rhubarb
- 5/8 cup of sugar 125g
- 1 cup of heavy cream 250 ml
- 1 lb strawberries
- 2-1/2 Ounces meringues 75g, small and large ones, work equally well
- lemon balm leaves for garnish

Instructions

1. Trim, peel, and cut the rhubarb stalks. While stirring continuously, bring the rhubarb and 1/3 cup of sugar to a boil in a pot. Cook the mixture for 7 to 10 minutes or until the rhubarb is exceptionally tender. Allow the mix to cool.
2. Cold rhubarb puree should be gently folded into the hard cream after whipping it.
3. Slice and clean the strawberries, saving some for garnish. Mix the remaining sugar with the strawberries.

4. Break up giant meringues into tiny pieces when using them. Layer the meringues, strawberries, and rhubarb cream in 4-6 serving glasses (or a big trifle basin). Serve the trifle immediately after garnishing it with the remaining strawberries and lemon balm.

SWEET VENISON CAKE

Ingredients

- 9 Ounces Zwieback biscuits
- 9 tbsp butter
- 5 Ounces of sugar
- Four eggs
- 3-1/2 Ounces ground almonds
- 2 tbsp flour
- 1 tsp baking powder

For the garnish:

- 3-1/2 Ounces dark chocolate
- 2 tbsp coconut oil
- 2 Ounces almonds for garnish

Instructions

1. Set the oven to 350°F/180°C for preheating. Grate the Zwieback very finely. Butter and sugar should be bubbly after beating.
2. Until the sugar is dissolved, add the eggs one at a time.
3. Mix the flour, baking powder, and powdered almonds with the Zwieback crumbs. Stir the mixture gradually into the creamy one.
4. Pour the batter into the baking pan after greasing and flouring it.
5. Bake for about 35 minutes at 350°F/180°C.
6. When the "venison" has had a chance to cool slightly, remove it from the pan and set it aside to cool.
7. Chop the chocolate for the glaze, then melt it with the coconut oil in a double boiler set over hot water. Garnish the cake.
8. To make the "venison" easy to cut into 18 pieces, insert the slivered almonds into the meat regularly.

GERMAN FRUIT FLAN RECIPE

Ingredients

- 6 tbsp (48 grams) all-purpose flour
- 6 tbsp (78 grams) granulated sugar (or 5 tbsp granulated sugar and 1 tbsp vanilla sugar
- 1 tsp (4 gram) baking powder
- Three large eggs
- filling and glaze

INSTRUCTIONS

1. oven to 360°F (182°C) before using.
2. Butter an 11-inch flan pan.
3. In a large basin, mix the flour, sugar, baking powder, and eggs. Using an electric mixer, beat the ingredients for 3 to 5 minutes or until they are light and fluffy.
4. Pour the batter carefully into the prepared tin.
5. 18 to 20 minutes of baking time, or until golden brown.
6. Allow to cool for about five minutes on the rack. Before filling, turn out onto a wire rack and let cool completely.

KOKOSMAKRONEN (GERMAN COCONUT MACAROONS)

INGREDIENTS

- 120g coconut flakes
- 250g sugar
- 4egg whites
- 30g flour
- baking wafers (4 cm in diameter)
- 1/2lemon, zest of, grated
- chocolate frosting (for decoration) (optional)

Instructions

1. Make a bath of water. Water should only faintly boil.
2. Mix sugar and egg whites in a bowl. After mixing to dissolve the sugar, submerge the bowl in the hot water bath.

3. Mix in the coconut flakes. Use a cooking thermometer to measure the temperature and stir the coconut mixture often as it is heated to 70 C.
4. Remove from the water bath, then stir in flour one more. You can add the shredded lemon peel to this mixture if you'd like.
5. Allow to once more very room temperature.
6. Set the oven to 160°C.
7. Baked goods are put on a baking sheet.
8. To apply little dough dollops on the wafers, use an icing bag with a large aperture. Because the cookies will somewhat flatten when baking, leave a small rim.
9. For ten minutes, bake. Then bake for a further 5 minutes with the oven slightly ajar.
10. The cookies should continue to be white and barely browned.
11. If you'd like, you can use chocolate icing to adorn the Kokosmakronen.
12. NOTE: To prepare the chocolate for decoration, melt two-thirds of it in a water bath. Remove from the water bath and stir in the remaining chocolate. Just heat it once more to melt the chocolate. Using an icing bag, sprinkle chocolate over the cookies or dip Kokosmakronen into it.
13. WARNING: If you don't have wafers on hand, you can spoon the dough directly on baking paper, but it might be challenging to remove the cookies from it later because they stick to it.

EASY GERMAN RUM BALLS (RUMKUGELN)

Ingredients

- 7 Tbsp [3.5 Ounces / 100g] unsalted butter (room temperature)
- ¾ cup of + [90 g+] powdered sugar
- 2 TBSP rum
- 7Ounces [200g] good chocolate, a mix of milk and dark
- 7Ounces [200g] hazelnuts
- 2 Tbsp cocoa powder, chocolate jimmies, sprinkles, hazelnuts, or powdered sugar (for rolling)

Instructions

1. Melt chocolate in a bowl set over a pan of hot water, a double boiler, or the microwave. Let the chocolate cool after it has melted.

2. Toast hazelnuts for 10 to 15 minutes at 350°F/176°C if using. Grind the skins in a food processor by pulsing them after removal.
3. Sifted powdered sugar and room-temperature butter should be creamed till light and fluffy.
4. Incorporate rum and cooled chocolate. Several times scrape down the sides as you blend to ensure smoothness. If you're adding ground hazelnuts, do it right away and mix well.
5. For 30 minutes, put the chocolate rum mixture in the refrigerator to chill. Note: Add extra powdered sugar and stir well if the chocolate mixture is not hard enough to form into balls after cooling. If you'd like, you can also incorporate a little chocolate powder.
6. Make 30 to 50 balls out of the chocolate rum mixture, and then roll everyone in cocoa powder or chocolate sprinkles.
7. For up to a week, keep in the refrigerator in an airtight container.

AUTHENTIC GERMAN CHEESECAKE

Ingredients

Crust

- 1-1/2 Cup of s [180g] flour
- 1 tsp baking powder
- pinch of salt
- 2 tsp vanilla sugar
- 1 tbsp finely grated lemon rind
- 1/4 cup of [50g] granulated sugar
- 6 TBSP [85g] butter
- One egg (beaten)

Filling

- Three egg yolks
- 3/4 Cup of [150g] granulated sugar
- 2 tsp vanilla sugar
- 6 TBSP [85g] butter (room temp)
- 3/4 cup of [170ml] heavy cream
- 2 Cup of s [450g] plain Quark

- 1-1/2 tsp cornstarch
- Three egg whites
- pinch of salt

Instructions

Crust

1. Mix the flour sifted with the baking powder, salt, sugar, and vanilla extract or sugar.
2. Butter should be cut in. Add the beaten egg, after which make a dough with your hands.
3. Refrigerate the dough for an hour after wrapping it in plastic.
4. Form a disc out of the cold dough, and then roll it out on a floured board. Roll the dough out twice after reshaping it into a disc. The dough was initially quite crumbly and challenging for me, but once I rolled it out twice, it was much more straightforward.
5. Once more rolling out the dough, please place it in a prepared 9-inch springform pan. (For instructions on folding and moving the dough to the springform pan, see the photographs above.) With your fingertips, push the dough into an even layer that extends up the sides and over the bottom of the pan.

Filling

1. Until pale, mix the egg yolks, sugar, and vanilla sugar. Continue beating after adding softened butter until everything is incorporated. Beat again after adding the heavy cream. Once everything is thoroughly blended, add quark (or Greek yogurt or pureed cottage cheese).
2. In a separate bowl, beat salt and egg whites until firm peaks form. Cheesecake batter should be combined with sifted cornstarch and egg whites.
3. Bake cheesecake batter at 300°F for about 60 minutes in a 9-inch springform pan. (I required 70 minutes to bake my cheesecake.) A toothpick inserted into the cheesecake should come out clean when baking. It's natural for the cheesecake's core to be a little wobbly and to fall as it cools.

4. After an hour on the counter, let the cheesecake chill for several hours in the refrigerator. Making this cheesecake the day before serving is recommended. Enjoy!

SPAGHETTI ICE CREAM

Ingredients

- Your favorite vanilla ice cream
- 8 Ounces of Strawberries quartered
- 1 tbsp of Sugar
- 2 tsp of Orange Juice, optional
- White Chocolate shavings
- Whipped Cream optional

Instructions

1. Place your serving utensils, potato rice, and freezer until thoroughly chilled.
2. Place the quartered strawberries in a blender along with the sugar. It extracts additional juices and allows it to sit for 5 to 10 minutes. If using, add orange juice, and mix for 5 minutes. Put the jar of sauce in the refrigerator to chill. White chocolate, which you should reserve.
3. Put two to three scoops of ice cream, or as much as wanted, into a potato ricer and press firmly to release the ice cream noodles onto a serving dish. Add strawberry sauce and white chocolate shavings to the top.
4. Serve right away and delight in!

PRINTABLE RECIPE BELOW

Ingredients

- 2 cups of sugar
- 1-1/2 cup of vegetable oil
- Two eggs
- 1/2 cup of molasses
- 4 cups of all-purpose flour
- Four tsp. baking soda
- 1 TBSP. ground ginger (powder)
- 2 tsp. ground cinnamon

- 1 tsp. salt
- Additional sugar

For dipped cookies:

- Two pkg. (12 oz. each) vanilla baking chips
- 1/4 cup of shortening (Crisco)

For drizzle-glaze cookies:

- 2 cups of powdered sugar
- 1-2 tsp. warm water
- 1 tsp. vanilla

Instructions

1. Turn the oven on to 350 degrees.
2. Oil and sugar should be thoroughly combined in a large mixing dish. One at a time beat well after every addition of an egg. Add molasses and stir.
3. Mix the dry ingredients in a separate bowl, then gradually add them to the creamed mixture while thoroughly combining them.
4. Roll the dough between your hands to make a 3/4-inch ball, and then roll the ball of cookie dough in sugar—approximately 1/3 cup, more or less—in a small bowl.
5. Place cookies on ungreased baking sheets 2 inches apart.
6. Bake for 10 to 12 minutes at 350 degrees or until the cookie bounces when lightly touched. Cookie removal and cooling on wire racks.
7. Depending on your preference, you can either dip the cookies or sprinkle a slight glaze over them once they have cooled. ENJOY!
8. Melt the vanilla chips and shortening in a small pan over low heat to prepare for dipping. Shake or let the excess drip out after dipping the cookies halfway into the mixture. To harden, place on baking pans lined with foil or wax paper.
9. Pour warm water, vanilla extract, and powdered sugar into a small basin. Stir until the mixture resembles a thin glaze; if necessary, add additional sugar or water to adjust the consistency. To collect any ice that may drip off the cookies, place the cookies on a piece of foil. Apply the icing to the cookies' tops. Allow to harden.

LINZER COOKIES

Ingredients

- 1-1/2 cup of butter, room temperature
- 1 cup of granulated sugar
- 1 tsp vanilla extract
- 1/2 tsp kosher salt
- 3-1/2 cup of all-purpose flour
- 3/4 cup of raspberry
- 1/2 cup of powdered sugar

Instructions

1. Butter and sugar should be combined for two minutes at medium speed in a stand mixer basin with the paddle attachment. Salt and vanilla should be mixed thoroughly after being added.
2. Mixer should be set to low, then add the flour and mix until mixed.
3. The dough should be taken out, shaped into a disk, and wrapped in plastic. Refrigerate for a minimum of one hour.
4. Put parchment paper on a baking pan and set it aside.
5. To remove the chill, take the dough out of the fridge and let it sit for 10 minutes.
6. Roll the dough to a 1/4-inch thickness with a rolling pin on a spotless counter.
7. Use a 2-inch round biscuit or cookie cutter to cut out the dough. Cut out a circle (or other form) in the middle of half of the rounds. A small cookie cutter or the back of a piping tip can be used.
8. Place the prepared baking sheet in the freezer and then top with the dough.
9. The oven to 350 degrees Fahrenheit. Remove the baking sheet from the freezer and bake for 18 to 20 minutes, or until the edges are just beginning to turn golden, once the oven is preheated.
10. Place the cookie on a wire rack to finish cooling.
11. Spread about 1 tsp of preserves on the bottoms of the solid biscuits once they have cooled. The cut-out cookies should be lightly pressed on top of the preserves.
12. Dust powdered sugar over every cookie.

GERMAN RICE PUDDING - MILCHREIS

INGREDIENTS

- 4 cups of milk
- One ¼ cup of Arborio rice
- 4 tbsp. sugar
- 1 tbsp. butter
- 1 tsp. Vanilla paste or 1 tbsp. vanilla sugar/extract

For the topping

- 1 tsp. cinnamon
- 2 tbsp. sugar
- 2 tbsp. brown butter

INSTRUCTIONS

1. Melt the butter in a big pot over medium heat.
2. After adding, simmer the rice for a few minutes.
3. Pour in the milk, sugar, and vanilla essence.
4. While stirring, bring the mixture to a boil.
5. Put a lid on the pot and lower the heat to a shallow setting.
6. When virtually all of the liquid has been absorbed, stirring occasionally. This will take 20 to 30 minutes.
7. Prepare the brown butter and mix the cinnamon and sugar.
8. Serve cold with fresh berries, compote, or apple sauce, or serve hot with brown butter and cinnamon/sugar.

PFEFFERNUSSE GERMAN PEPPER NUT COOKIES

Ingredients

- 1/2 cup of softened butter
- 3/4 cup of light brown sugar
- 1/4 cup of molasses
- One egg
- 2-1/4 cup of s all-purpose flour
- 1/2 tsp baking soda
- 1/2 tsp kosher salt

- 1/2 tsp cinnamon
- 1/2 tsp anise seed as finely crushed as possible
- 1/2 tsp freshly ground black pepper
- 1/4 tsp ground nutmeg
- 1/4 tsp ground allspice
- 1/8 tsp ground cardamom
- 1/8 tsp ground cloves
- 1-1/2 cup of s powdered sugar

Instructions

1. In a sizable mixing basin, mash the butter, brown sugar, and molasses together until smooth. Beat in the egg after adding it. The spices, baking soda, and flour should be whipped together. Mix the dry components with the wet ones gradually before adding them together. The dough should be chilled in the fridge for at least one hour.

2. Turn the oven on to 350 degrees. Scoop some cookie dough and roll it between your palms to form a ball. On a baking sheet covered with parchment or silpat, place the dough balls. When firm to the touch, bake for 13–14 minutes. Take the cookies out of the oven and let them cool for three minutes on the baking sheets.

3. Put the powdered sugar in a lidded, medium-sized container. At a time, dunk a few cookies into the powdered sugar. Put a lid on top and gently shake to coat. Once completely cold, move the covered cookies to a wire cooling rack. Repeat with the remaining cookies. Use an airtight container for storage. Enjoy!

THE END

Printed in Great Britain
by Amazon

33657786-b0d8-49c0-b62e-354da795cd3aR02